Best wishes for
a "good read".
Sincerely,
Diane Brenda Bryan

SOLDIER
OF
GOD

a novel by

Diane Brenda Bryan

Pittsburgh, PA

ISBN 1-56315-247-9

Paperback Fiction
© Copyright 2002 Diane Brenda Bryan
All Rights Reserved
First Printing — 2001
Library of Congress #2001090116

Request for information should be addressed to: *me*

SterlingHouse Publisher, Inc.
The Sterling Building
440 Friday Road
Pittsburgh, PA 15209
www.sterlinghousepublisher.com

Book Designer: Beth Buckholtz
Cover Design: Michelle Lenkner — SterlingHouse Publisher, Inc.

This publication includes images from Corel Draw 8 which are
protected by the copyright laws of the U.S., Canada and elsewhere.

Printed in the United States of America

DEDICATION

To my loving, patient husband Jack and
my children: Jeffrey, Elyn and Jonathan, who cheered me on.

WITH GRATITUDE

To my colleagues at the Boca Raton Writers' Roundtable:
Bea Erwe, Mark Jacoby, Lotte Povar,
Donald Silverman and David Shapiro
for their criticism and comfort.

To Dr. Stanford M. Lyman at FAU for starting me on this journey.
To the American Jewish Historical Society for archival materials.
To the Old Testament.
To the New Testament.
To the Boca Raton Public Library and various university libraries.

I would rather be a sexton
In the house of the Lord
Than be emperor
Of this entire world.

Luis de Carvajal, the younger

CHAPTER 1

PROLOGUE TO DESTINY

"On this day, the 15th of February, in the year of our Lord, 1589, you are hereby summoned to appear before the High Tribunal of the Holy Office in Mexico City..." Governor Luis de Carvajal y de la Cueva held the official document in hands that trembled with rage. "What is the meaning of this?" he demanded of no one as he sat, a lone figure on horseback, on the rim of a hill overlooking miles and miles of land in all directions. This land had been granted to him by King Philip II of Spain who had designated him as governor.

Don Luis pushed his broad-brimmed black hat toward the back of his head where it hung at the base of his neck, suspended by a braided cordel. His long, black cape swung low to one side, exposing his scabbard and sword, the gold embroidered insignia of his office obvious on the left side of his cloak.

Dusk was rapidly approaching. The sky was tinged with streamers of a deep-hued orange as the sun was sinking. He continued to gaze at the vast territory called Nuevo Leon. He had earned this prize. Tilting his head to one side, he closed his eyes and relived in his mind battles fought hard on land and sea for Spain in this New World. He remembered that glorious day when he was given the title of Admiral because of his courage and valor in defeating Sir Alfred Drake, the English corsair, in a rival encounter in 1568, off the coast of Mexico. His tour de force included not only battling pirate ships but also natives he encountered during his land expeditions.

Courageous and ambitious, Don Luis, age 21, had come to this distant place, as had many fortune seekers, in the service of the King and Queen of Spain. Serving with Francesco Velasquez de Coronado, many new and distant territories were explored while they searched for the realm of fabled wealth — the Seven Cities of Cibola.

He recalled the feeling of futility and disappointment that overcame Coronado and his conquistadores when they finally were forced to accept the fact that there was no gold; only endless prairies and hostile natives. His conversation with Coronada that last night still remained vivid in his memory. As they sat before a crude fire, Coronada had said, sadly, "Luis, I fear we must turn back. There is nothing further to pursue."

"Sir, you have done your best. We all have. Do not be so disconsolate. It is not your fault that we did not find gold. Think of all the territories we have explored upon which flies the flag of Spain."

"Ah, yes, Don Luis. We have fought boldly and persevered, but it is time to go back. Too many have suffered and died already. There is no more to be accomplished here. We must halt our quest."

Don Luis could still feel the sorrow that overwhelmed him as he looked at the old warrior and tried to comfort him. "Your efforts will be noted and appreciated, I am sure. You are a valiant soldier of Spain."

"Prepare to return to Mexico," was all Coronado had answered.

* * *

A devout Catholic, the son of New Christians who had converted three generations back in Spain during the Inquisition, he knew little of the ways of the Old Religion and the Judaic laws. Raised in the Church, he assiduously practiced the Evangelical Law. His brother Domingo was a Jesuit. The governor knew that if the authorities suspected Jewish origins, he would not have been allowed to come to this new land or granted the right to own property. The Spanish decrees of 1501 and 1522 were familiar to him. These laws had established that only those of Catholic heritage could settle and own land in the Spanish colonies. Staunch in his observance and devotion to the Catholic Church, this had never been a concern of his.

His horse, growing restless, stirred beneath him, but Don Luis continued to reminisce. He thought how ironic it was that circumstances had reversed themselves because of a convolution of occurrences. Images spilled over in his memory as he visualized his return to Spain in 1578, after ten years of devoted service abroad. He had returned to convince King Philip II that the new lands he had claimed for the Royal Court should be placed under his control as governor, explaining, "I have overcome the hostility of many savage tribes who inhabit the area and who hate the Spanish. It is my fair treatment and bravery that have earned me the esteem and respect of both my soldiers and the natives. I have made great strides in achieving peace, Sire, at my own personal expense and danger."

The King, impressed, had urged, "Please tell me more about these lands."

In glowing terms, Don Luis had described the territory. "Your Majesty, it is a land of irregular patterns, of spectacular vistas of plateaus and mountain chains, set off by rich soil and desert. The temperatures vary from extreme hot to cold. It is a fertile land through which flow streams and rivers abounding with varieties of fish. Exotic herbs and trees grow in abundance, and animals roam the forests. But, best of all," here Don Luis paused dramatically, "thanks to the Lord, there are mines dotting the region — mines laden with silver, lead and copper — ready to yield a fortune."

Animated by the good news, the King had exclaimed, "Well done, Don Luis. I shall proceed with plans to install you as Governor of Nuevo Leon."

His horse shifted again uneasily, but the governor ignored it, continuing with his ruminating. Recalling the reunion with his wife and her family on their beautiful estate *La Pajeria* (The Straw Loft), brought a smile to his face. Had it really been ten years since he had last been home? Enthusiasm for his career as a conquistador and now the soon-to-be Governor of Nuevo Leon brought pride to his loved ones. He was carrying on in the true tradition of the de Carvajals. His happiness at being reunited with the family was two-pronged: he had longed to come home to see them, but now he had an ulterior motive as well. The land of which he would be governor would require trusted friends and family to administrate and colonize it.

Don Luis had spoken at great length to his wife and family, as well as to other relatives, drawing rosy and irresistible pictures. Seeking out relatives, he often visited different towns, using all of his persuasive powers to enlist them in joining him on his return voyage. He made many ardent promises. "Amigos, come join in the adventure," he had urged. Those whom he had convinced were told to wait until they received word from him. "Then we shall proceed with the final plans." All had depended upon the formal edict from the King, formally installing him as governor of the new lands.

He recalled the long six months of waiting until, finally, on May 31st, 1579, Philip II issued the charter naming Don Luis de Carvajal as Governor of Nuevo Leon, in "recognition of his desire to be of service to our Lord and ourselves." The King had further stipulated that as a conquistador and a governor, Don Luis had the privilege of bequeathing his estate to a son or other heir of his choosing. Surprisingly, he had further decreed that the entourage traveling with the governor was exempted from any investigation of family lineage.

Don Luis absent-mindedly patted his horse's flanks. He wondered now why he had been so foolish as not to recognize the importance and gravity of this release. Musing aloud, he said, "I was too happy, I suppose. My mission had succeeded and my status was assured. My occasional suspicions about family practices did not concern me. The important thing at that moment was to convince Guiomar, my wife, and my sister and her family to join me." He sighed as he recalled the conversation with his brother-in-law, Don Francisco. "Leave Medina del Campo, come with me and you will all live on my land. There is much wealth to be had. You will want for nothing."

Already planning to take his family to France, Don Francisco had replied, "I do not know. It is hard to make such a decision. What do I know of the New World?"

"Francisco, you and yours will live in a fine house and make a good living, under my protection." He had placed his arm around his brother-in-law's shoulders and said, affectionately, "Come, come, my brother. If you join me, I shall give your son Luis Rodriquez my name and he shall be my heir. You know Guiomar and I have no children."

The offer to make Young Luis his heir was something Francisco had found difficult to refuse and, after a moment's reflection, he had shaken Don Luis' hand.

Not everyone had agreed to go. Don Luis recalled his devastation when his wife refused to go. She was a "crypto-Jew" (secret Jew) and she was as devout in her faith as he was in his. Outwardly, she was Catholic in every respect and attended church regularly. He had always been suspicious of her activities, however, and feared that she might be a Judaizer. Her refusal to join him had rekindled his mistrust, a mistrust that hung over his head like a sword of Damocles. All the old devils had stirred within him and, if he was to have any peace of mind, he knew he had to convince her to accompany him. With her close by, he hoped to control any clandestine practices. He had been afraid, with the increased activity of the Holy Office of the Inquisition, that should any scrutiny of the family's descent arise, there could be a problem.

He had portrayed life in the New World in glowing terms in the hope of enticing her but to no avail. Not realizing at the time how important it was to her that she stay with the family, who all practiced the Old Religion in secret, he had begged her to come to the "land of paradise" — conveniently omitting the fact that the Office of the Inquisition had been instituted in Mexico, in November of 1571.

Don Luis' horse grew more restless and lifted his head as if to question his master. Stroking the animal's mane, Don Luis promised, "Only a few more memories, amigo."

The scene at the dock had been a tumultuous one. He recalled tears of sorrow mingling with the joy of anticipation. Once again, he remembered Francisco's voice pleading as he hugged his sister-in-law, "Will you not reconsider? Your husband has achieved great status and wealth. Life will be sweet for you."

"Do not worry," she had answered. "I shall manage very well. My parents and my cousins are devoted to me." She kissed him on the cheek. "Goodbye, my dear one. I hope we shall see each other again. God be with all of you on this journey. I shall eagerly await news of the de Carvajals."

Don Francisco, distraught, had kissed her one more time and turned to collect his family's belongings and the mementos of his life. Don Luis had been thankful for his efforts to influence Guiomar.

The travelers had all huddled together, young and old, their possessions at their feet or in their arms, and in their hearts, great hope. Many had come to the Port of Seville at great personal expense and discomfort, having traveled from distant towns, some staying with relatives along the way.

Don Francisco and Dona Francisca had stayed at la Pajeria. It had been a pleasant visit and a momentous one. Francisco's daughter Isabel had been living with Guiomar and her family since the death of her husband. Isabel had not seen the family for two years and now she would join them on the voyage.

Don Luis sighed. When a scene had ensued at the port! All those people converging to participate in the most daring adventure of their lives. Friendly greetings and familial expressions of love had been exchanged as they stood in clusters waiting to depart. They still echoed in his brain.

The large, wooden ship that would be home for endless days and nights creaked, swaying at the dock, waiting for its human cargo to board. The food and supplies, including fowl and livestock, had already been loaded into the hold. For the trip, each family had brought along jars of condiments and foodstuffs as well. The clucking of chickens and animal noises had mingled with the human sounds of excitement.

It had been a busy time. He had had to make sure that all the arrangements were proper. Such voyages were never easy enterprises. From past experience he had known that summer squalls could be treacherous and the possibility of violent winds was always imminent. He had not dared tell this to his family and the others. He had been sure that once the ship joined the summer fleet, they would enjoy a sense of security. Silently, he prayed to the Lord for safe delivery to their destination.

Bringing so many people to colonize new territories had been a feather in his cap and he had had great expectations about his sphere of influence. His mind began to wander back to the scene with his wife and how he had tried to convince her. Embracing her, he had asked, again, "Will you not come, Guiomar, my love? You know that as a soldier I must execute my contract with the King and fulfill the commission to which I was appointed. But, I need you by my side —"

She had stopped him by placing her fingers gently upon his lips. "*Mi corazon*, I must remain here. You know how fearful I am of such a trip and of the new lands of which I know nothing. God willing, we shall see each other again soon."

Reluctantly, he had kissed her tenderly on the forehead and then on her soft mouth, whispering a loving farewell. "*Adios, cara mia.*"

There was no time for further pleadings and endearments. The captain of the ship had signaled that they were ready to sail. He had ushered his pilgrims up the gangplank. Each in turn had looked back quickly to wave to those who had come to bid them farewell. A bell in the harbor intoned the departure of the vessel. The night was suddenly still except for the haunting sound of a guitar and a young, lilting voice. "*Adios, amigos, vaya con Dios,*" the lyrics rang out. "Goodbye, friends, go with God."

He remembered, too, how Francisco had pulled his son, Young Luis, to him and as he embraced him, had raised a fist in a sign of strength and determination and cried, "To a new life!"

CHAPTER II

THE VOYAGE

June 10th, 1580. Governor de Carvajal's ship, the *Nuestra Senora de la Luz* (Our Lady of the Light), a large, four-masted galleon, was one of many built in the 16th-century to be used as warships or traders. Spain employed these vessels in her conquests, from the Americas to the distant Philippines.

A sizable vessel was needed to accommodate the impressive numbers of the Governor's entourage. Ever since the King had conferred the title upon Don Luis, everything he did rated special attention. What stature he had achieved! He was Governor of the New Kingdom of Leon, a territory that extended from Tampico to San Antonio and ranged 600 miles inland from the Gulf of Mexico.

As the ship departed from the harbor of Seville, the Governor stood next to his First Mate and observed, "We have a clear night and a good wind at our backs. A fortuitous omen, indeed."

The helmsman agreed and added, "If we are not confronted by pirate ships or a norte, all will go well."

Don Luis slapped him on the back and jokingly suggested, "We should worry more about the *teredos*, my friend. We can fight pirates and strong winds, but we are helpless at an attack from these mollusks. They can eat right through a wooden hull. But, not to worry, amigo — this ship is sheathed with lead. That should take the sting out of the bite, eh?" Privately, the Governor hoped so for he was well aware that sheathing enjoyed a limited success.

A guitar was heard being played softly in the sailors' quarters. Stars shone brightly in the blackness surrounding them. Don Luis inquired about the schedule for the night watch and then retired below to visit his passengers. He found his flock gathered in little clusters around lighted candles.

"My beloved family and friends, the Lord in His mercy smiles upon us for we have calm waters, a fine westerly wind, and bright stars to guide us. Let us pray together to give thanks."

There were sounds of agreement and all fell to their knees.

The governor was in high spirits and soon he sought out his brother-in-law, Don Francisco. "Come join me for some brandy and we shall talk."

Francisco quickly came to his side, anxious to find out more about their destination. When they were seated in the galley and at the governor's request, one of the crew brought a bottle of brandy and two glasses.

Questions began to spill out of Francisco. "I should like to know so much about this New Spain, this Mexico to which we go. What is the land like? Can it be farmed? Are there schools for the children? Is there danger from the natives...?"

Don Luis interrupted. "Francisco, so many concerns! Be at peace. You will have good land and a fine house. As for any danger — some of the finest soldiers of Spain will protect you."

Francisco felt foolish for showing uneasiness and a lack of confidence and he immediately apologized. "I know you will do the best for us, Don Luis. I deeply regret my poor manners."

"*De nada*," answered the governor. "I will say good night now. Sleep well and do not worry yourself."

A brilliant morning ushered in a day of much activity. The crew was busy trimming the sails and doing all the necessary chores to keep the ship seaworthy. The passengers were scurrying about from stem to stern, like children on an adventure — one they had never imagined they would be experiencing. Now, in broad daylight, they were able to peek into every nook and cranny and ask a multitude of questions about all the contraptions and new objects that surrounded them. There was so much to talk about. The air was filled with a plethora of voices.

At first, the weather had been surprisingly reliable. It seemed that even Mother Nature had conveyed her blessings upon them. But then there came days when a grayish veil hung over everything — gray clouds, gray seas, no sign of the horizon, the sun shining pale as through frosted glass. Often a dark layer would obliterate the sun and totally blacken the sky. The travelers quickly learned that these signs indicated that a *norte* was imminent. Thunder, followed by cataracts of lightning, would shatter the air. The winds would tear across the expanse of sky and whip the water into a frenzy. Frightened, the passengers would spend their time praying that the Lord bring them to safe harbor.

Not only were the weather conditions unbearable a good deal of the time, but daily life became more and more difficult, particularly because of the lack of sanitary conditions.

Young Luis, who would later be known as Luis de Carvajal, *el mozo* (the younger), was one of seven siblings of Francisca and Francisco de Matos. He was approaching his thirteenth birthday. Thus far, his education had been in Jesuit schools where he had proved to be an outstanding student. All of his life he had gone to church every Sunday and practiced the tenets of Catholicism. Late one night, during the voyage, he observed his mother and sister Isabel engaging in prayers and rituals unfamiliar to him. When he questioned his father, Don Francisco had answered, "I will explain some things to you very soon. We have much to talk about."

Young Luis wondered when and what that could be. Meanwhile, he became more curious about the strange practices of his family. Having been instructed in Catholicism, he could not identify any observances he witnessed.

On one particular stormy night, as Luis snuggled against his father, he could hear his mother and sister softly singing hymns. Francisco looked down at his son and, as if in answer to the boy's questioning glances, he said, "I believe it is time to reveal something of great importance to you. We are going to a new land, to a new life, and I want us to live it in truth, with honor."

The boy could not imagine what his father was about to tell him.

"My son, you are a Jew and I want you to learn what that means. Your mother and sister Isabel have secretly clung to the God of the Law of Moses..."

"The God of the Law of Moses?" Luis interrupted. "What does all this mean? My oldest brother, Gaspar, is a priest. All my life I have listened to stories of the family's accomplishments in the name of the King and the Church. What of my grandfather, who was a conquistador and a judge? My uncle, who was an advisor to the Royal Court? Even you, Father — you served the Count de Benevente." He was really confused. The family always attended church regularly and recited the Hail Marys. Don Francisco had been a respected merchant in the Christian community of Benavente and later, when they moved to Medina del Campo, they had prospered and were an integral part of that town as well. What did his father's revelation mean?

Don Francisco painfully described how, under the rule of the Inquisition, it was necessary to convert to the Church in order to remain in Spain. "Many converted in order to save their lives. They did not want to leave Spain or Portugal; they loved their homeland, but to stay without converting meant imprisonment and, often, death. They became New Christians — *"conversos"* — who secretly worshipped the Old Religion, but outwardly practiced

Catholicism. These "converso" families often sent a son in service to the Church, as we did with your brother Gaspar, to maintain appearances."

Luis was aghast at the unfolding story. Father and son sat late into the night, exchanging questions and answers until, finally exhausted, they fell asleep — the boy propped up in the circle of his father's arms. Before he fell asleep, his last question to his father had been, "What of Uncle Luis? Is he a Secret Jew, too?" and, from the look on his father's face, he understood that he must not speak of what had been revealed to him.

The following morning, the sun shone upon them and the voyagers once again walked the decks, socializing, speculating about the trip. Don Francisco brought Young Luis to Dr. Manuel de Morales. "My son, the doctor is well versed in the Old Religion. You will spend time with him to receive instruction in the principles of Judaism, the Mosaic Law." From that moment on, Luis' life changed dramatically.

Dr. Morales was not only a physician, but a learned scholar as well. It was not too long before the boy became an ardent disciple. His parents were overjoyed. It had worried them that he might rebel because, after all, his entire education had been in Catholic schools.

A flood of questions from the neophyte dominated his first meeting with the doctor. Who is the God of the Law of Moses? What is the Law? The doctor patiently explained, "Adonai is God, and the Law of Moses is His Law. It must be adhered to and those who believe will find salvation and eternal life in the hereafter."

Luis became increasingly enthralled. It was obvious to him that the doctor held the Lord in great awe and was a devoted servant. Together they discussed the Old Testament and its traditions. "Maintaining the Sabbath," Dr. Morales instructed, "was honoring God's wondrous work and His rest on the seventh day, Saturday."

This puzzled Luis. He had always been told that Sunday was the Sabbath day.

His mentor continued. "The tradition of the Sabbath is described in the second chapter of the Bible. 'And God blessed the seventh day and declared it holy, because on it God ceased from all the work of creation that He had done'. Later, the Fourth Commandment ordained that Israel 'remember the Sabbath day to make it holy'."

He continued to speak of other sacred days. Luis showed great interest in the Great Day and asked, "When is that Day?"

"It is observed on the eighth day following the celebration of Rosh ha-Shana, the New Year. In fact, if we arrive at our destination as scheduled it will be almost time to observe those holy days."

Intrigued, Luis encouraged the doctor to continue.

"A harvest festival called Sukkot comes five days after the Great Day. The Israelites were commanded to build temporary booths where they would stay for a week and take all their meals. Most ate in the 'sukkot', but slept in their homes."

"This is all so new and fascinating. Please continue," the boy urged.

"About the time that Easter is celebrated by Christians, we celebrate Passover (Pascua) in memory of God's deliverance of the children of Israel from Egyptian bondage." He continued to describe the circumstances and the significance of the 'matzot' (the unleavened bread), and then Dr. Morales told Luis, "I think we have studied enough for today. Join your family. I shall see you tomorrow. You are a fine lad."

Days passed, filled with endless stories about Biblical heroes and heroines and of wicked tyrants and despots like the evil Haman, Prime Minister of Persia. Luis hungrily absorbed every detail. Unfortunately, Luis became ill but he refused to miss a single day of instruction. Now that he had an understanding of what his mother and sister were doing, he often joined them in prayer at night. Francisco told him, "I am so happy that you have so willingly embraced your new-found roots."

The otherwise uneventful journey took about two and one-half months. The ship made a stop at Gomera in the Canary Islands on June 19, where they joined the Summer Fleet, to replenish supplies and make necessary repairs. They set sail again on the 23rd. The opportunity to go ashore was welcomed by the weary travelers. After a layover of four days, they were on their way and reached Desirade by July 15th. The next stop was Ocoa where they picked up more supplies and separated from those ships which had been assigned to remain in the Indies.

Traveling as part of a fleet provided them with protection from the corsairs that roamed the open seas attacking Spanish vessels for their cargoes of gold bullion and other valuables. English and French pirate ships often lay in wait, ready to assault and plunder. Governor de Carvajal had no fear of such engagements. Our Lady of the Light was one of the finest ships afloat, with a well-manned crew and equipped to meet any exigency. Manpower and weaponry were more than adequate.

When Luis heard about the possibility of pirate attacks — hyper-imaginative as he was — he fantasized about heroic battles in which he stood by his uncle's side with scabbard in hand, bravely and victoriously defending his family, repelling all boarders — a conquistador at heart, with God's name upon his lips.

The Summer Fleet entered the Port of San Juan de Uluam, off the mainland of Veracruz, on August 25, 1580. At the head of the convoy was the lead ship, displaying the royal colors and the insignia of the captain general. In the rear of the convoy sailed the vice-admiral's ship, ready to resist any challenges.

The arrival of Spanish ships to any port in New Spain always generated great excitement. When the distant sails of the vessels were spotted, a salute was fired from the mainland to which the lead ship responded with appropriate salvos. People gathered along the shore to welcome the newcomers. Our Lady of the Light continued on to the port of Tampico on the Panuco River, in accordance with the governor's plans. His group of emigres was now a sorry-looking lot having suffered through, for the most part, various sieges of dysentery, vertigo, and seasickness during the voyage. Luis' mother, Dona Francisca, had helped care for Dr. Morales' sister who was ill, but because of poor conditions and lack of medication, she succumbed. Luis was lucky because the doctor was able to help him medically as well as spiritually. The lessons in Judaism continued every day. The governor, concerned about his nephew's health, heartily welcomed the doctor's devoted attention.

Tampico, September 3rd, 1580. As the de Carvajals waited on deck for the ship to dock, they peered out at the land they would soon call home. The scene that greeted them was disturbing. In what appeared to be a clearing in a thickly forested, dank area, stood some old adobes made of brick, sun-dried clay, and straw — the most common building material used in New Spain. The foliage surrounding the houses was comprised mainly of fruit trees. Strategically placed were a fortress and a crude, thatch-roofed church. The area looked like a swampland.

Francisco, sheltering a dozing Luis in his arms, turned angrily to his wife. After a swift intake of breath, an invective escaped his lips. "*Merdoso! Dios mio,* where has your brother taken us? We have come from purgatory to hell!"

Dona Francisca inwardly fearful that the governor had duped them, nevertheless attempted to pacify her husband. "Please, dear — calm yourself. I am sure Don Luis will explain that we are merely stopping here for a little while because so many are not well. Maybe the change from sea to land will help our son to feel better."

He retorted, "I have a bad feeling about this. Your brother has tricked us."

She could not help but agree. A wave of hopelessness swept over her and as she looked around at the faces of others, she saw similar signs of despair and disappointment. Francisca was glad that Luis was asleep and not as yet witness to this scene of desolation. The rest of the family stood by silently. Francisca told them all to pray to God for divine guidance.

As the group disembarked, there were cries of protest. This was far from the Promised Land described by the governor. Surely it was nothing like the glowing pictures painted by adventurers upon their return to the Iberian Peninsula!

Sensing their agitation, Don Luis hastened to assuage the disgruntled group. "My family and friends, for a very short time you shall stay here. Your needs will be attended to and some soldiers will remain with you for your protection against any native attacks." The governor knew how dangerous the Panuco area was and now he saw the fear on the faces before him. "I have explained to you that I have discovered some beautiful rich land that shows much promise. The King has made me governor of that territory and soon you shall all live there comfortably, but first I must go there with my men to bring about further pacification of the natives. The King has named it *Nuevo Leon* and soon you will colonize it. Prosperity awaits you and great opportunities for a rich life. Have patience and you will be rewarded."

His earnestness had a soothing affect upon most of them, yet Francisca and Francisco were unable to suppress twinges of distrust.

CHAPTER III

THE COVENANT

After the travelers' belongings were unloaded and families claimed their baggage, they were assigned to adobe houses. Personal property was stored separately, where necessary, in small shacks. That first night was a horror. A ferocious storm hit the area and destroyed some of the wooden buildings, including the one in which Luis and his brother Baltasar were spending the night. They had volunteered to sleep there to guard the de Carvajal's supplies and personal items. A fierce wind tore a path through the little town, leveling some structures, collapsing walls and tearing roofs away. As the boys listened to the threatening sounds, they shuddered and huddled in a corner. When the wind began battering the walls with threatening force, they decided to make a run for it. Miraculously, they escaped just as the building crumbled into a spiral of timbers and twisted roof.

"By the mercy of God," Dona Francisca cried out when she saw her sons racing toward the house. She held each one tightly, uttering profuse exclamations of gratitude to the Lord, for surely they had survived only through His intervention. Her prayers ran the gamut from the "blessed saints" to the "Almighty God of Israel." She thanked them all, as did Francisco and the other children.

"Son, you have been spared together with your brother to do great things in this new land. You will be a soldier of God and will bring back the Law of Moses to our people." Francisco discussed with the two boys the possibility of reconverting some of the New Christians who had come there. "Luis, you are extremely bright and you learn quickly. Already your fervor for the practice of Judaism is great. With your convincing ways, you will be a worthy teacher of the Mosaic Law."

Eagerly, Luis responded, "Father, there is nothing I would rather do. I am intoxicated by the oneness of the God of Israel and I shall devote my life to Him." He said this with so much sincerity that it brought tears to his parents' eyes.

"But," cautioned his father, "we must be extremely careful. Your uncle does not appreciate any demonstration of what he calls a 'deplorable purblind condition'. This is how refers to those who he believes are 'blind' in matters of faith — his faith."

As the difficult days of adjusting to their new environs passed, Luis became more and more passionate about his studies. He gleaned information from every possible source. One day, he was fortunate enough to buy a Bible from a visiting monk. After some extensive reading, he realized that, in his classes in Jesuit school, all information concerning the Jews had been deleted from their texts. Thank God he had the prayer book and original supplications which Dr. Morales had used to indoctrinate him. All this reading material only whetted his appetite. There was much to study and he relished the task.

The small, confining house to which the de Carvajals were assigned was a far cry from the one in which they had lived in Medina del Campo in Portugal. The old town had been a beehive of activity. Business flourished because of a thriving trade with Europe of manufactured fabrics. Don Francisco had prospered in his little shop on Salamanca Street and the family had lived comfortably. When Seville, a city to the south of them, became a big trading center, business in Medina del Campo depreciated considerably. It was at that time that he began contemplating a move to France. Fate, however, in the guise of Governor de Carvajal, had intervened.

Now here they were in a strange, distant land in which, so far, not a ray of hope shone through the veil of dismal circumstances. Life proved to be difficult. The land was not good for farming, and there was little going on insofar as industry and trade. The de Carvajals lived at the poverty level, while Don Francisco, Luis and Baltasar tried to conduct some business peddling miscellaneous household items in the village and nearby towns. Even the weather was not consolation, running extremes from intense heat to severe winter nortes. In this sorry state, the family clung tenaciously to their faith, determined that salvation would be the justification for their suffering.

Near the end of 1581, when Dr. Morales and his wife left Mexico to return to Europe, Baltasar was designated by his parents to continue with Luis' religious instruction. He was the older of the two and fairly well-versed in some of the Judaic doctrines. Luis was an eager student. The boy's appetite for stories and information was insatiable. The brothers spent endless hours exploring religious dogma when they were not otherwise engaged in business activities.

While sitting alone one day reading Chapter 17 of the Book of Revelations, Luis came across the story of the circumcision of Abraham at the age of 99. The account fascinated him because he knew nothing of this ritual. He and his brothers had not been circumcised. When he read Genesis 17:14, "And the uncircumcised male who is not circumcised in the flesh of his foreskin, that soul shall be cut off from his people; he hath broken my covenant," it left him in a highly emotional state. His reaction was that the condition had to be rectified immediately if his name were to be written with those of his people in God's book. Grabbing a pair of scissors from his mother's sewing kit, Luis decided he would perform the ritual himself. He ran from the house, down to the banks of the Panuco. *To find salvation*, he thought, *I must keep this covenant with God.*

Far from being the adept surgeon, the boy unskillfully removed a larger portion of his foreskin than was necessary. While crying out in pain, he exhorted God to bless him as a believer. The experience was a passionate one. It exhausted him. After several minutes, he washed himself by the side of the river and then returned to the house where he applied a clean cloth to the wound. A feeling of oneness with God overwhelmed him and he sank to his knees, begging, "Oh, Lord, accept my deed of good intention as my deep desire to serve and love You all the days of my life."

Baltasar found his brother later that day resting on his bed, weakened by the trauma.

"Brother," Luis called to him. "I have done God's will."

"And what was that?" Baltasar asked.

"I have circumcised myself!" Luis drew aside the covers and exposed the fresh cut.

Baltasar was horrified. "What have you done to yourself?"

When Luis explained what he had read in the Bible and showed him the passages, his brother vowed to do the same during the coming Passover, in the spring of 1582. This he did and even though he used a razor, his skill was even less than that of Luis' and his recuperation took much longer. When he was healed, the boys told their mother what both had done. Even though Francisca had her reservation about the wisdom of such an act — so obviously a Jewish practice — she embraced them both and blessed them. Then she scolded them good-naturedly for not allowing her to care for them.

"Come, this is a cause for celebration," she declared. "We shall have dinner and spend the Sabbath together singing hymns and praising the Lord."

The boys gazed upon their mother with great love. Surely, she must be one of God's favorites! they agreed. Francisca was truly a kind and loving woman, devoid of any vanity or wickedness.

In preparation for the Sabbath, Francisca and her daughters had cleaned the house, changed bed clothes, and cooked a festive meal, the remains of which would be kept warm overnight for the next day, Saturday, when no chores or cooking was allowed. They bathed, clipped their nails, and dressed in their best on Friday nights. A homemade candle was lit in remembrance of dear, departed souls. Sabbath nights always required extra caution. Doors were kept locked in case someone unexpected came to the house. There was always the fear of their rituals being overheard. In that respect, they were careful to recite cleverly improvised hymns that were chanted or sung in Latin or Spanish.

That Friday night was a wonderfully happy one. The meal had been prepared in the traditional manner, and the fowl had been slaughtered according to Jewish dietary laws. After the soup, the *"roz con pollo"* (chicken with rice) with side dishes of potato cakes, spinach pies, and vegetables was followed by a variety of fruits and baked delicacies. Appetites and spirits rose to the challenge.

A sudden knock at the door brought an abrupt end to the gaiety. Everyone tensed. Francisco hastened to unlock the door and carefully opened it. Governor de Carvajal stood in the entrance.

"Oh, Don Luis, come in, come in. We were just reminiscing about our homeland. You are just in time for some brandy and coffee."

The governor greeted everyone and made himself comfortable. "I have good news," he announced. "I am returning to Nuevo Leon next week, and Young Luis shall accompany me. It is time my namesake and heir learned something about pacifying the natives and ruling the territory that he will inherit someday. I have sent the necessary documents to the Spanish Court naming him second in command."

Luis noticed his mother tried to disguise the apprehension he knew she was feeling.

"So soon, Don Luis? There is much work to be done here and he is needed to help his father conduct business —"

"Do not be foolish, my sister. As heir to my holdings, he must become familiar with the responsibilities of the *encomenderos*. He must learn how a landowner oversees his land and the natives who work it. How else will he be ready to take my place when the time comes?" The governor gulped down another brandy.

Luis wondered how he would continue his secret studies and meetings if he joined his uncle but he said nothing. The agitation on the faces of his parents was painful to him. As much as he wanted to stay, he knew it was crucial that he accompany the governor. It would arouse curiosity if he insisted that he remain in Tampico, so he nodded to his mother and father, saying, "Uncle Luis is right. I shall be a conquistador and ride by his side. I must learn about the land and the ways of the Indians so that we may live in peace."

Don Luis put his arm around his nephew and said with evident pride, "This boy already understands his role. He is smart, an asset to me, to all of us. My dear family you shall be prosperous. Life will be sweet."

Dona Francisca looked at her brother and thought, *So far there has been very little sugar in the pot*. But more than that, she was worried about her son going to the wilderness and all of its potential dangers. She looked lovingly at Luis — not yet sixteen — and wanted to hold him tightly to her heart and never let go, but she could not afford even a fleeting display of fear or doubt.

Her husband poured out more brandy. "Come, come, all of you. This is an occasion for rejoicing. A new conquistador is in the making." He kissed his son. "You are bright and courageous and you shall make us proud. May the Lord bless you." Turning to the others, he lifted his glass and said, "We shall drink a toast to the governor and his namesake." Glasses were raised and all beseeched God to keep their "brave soldiers" from harm.

After coffee, Don Luis excused himself. "The hour grows late and I have much preparation to make for our expedition. We shall probably spend many months establishing our control, so I must see to it that provisions are sufficient."

Luis interjected, "Uncle, am I to wear the uniform of a conquistador?"

"Of course, of course. I shall stop by tomorrow afternoon with the garments so that they may be fitted to you. I am sure your mother and sisters can handle that. Soon we shall go to the stables where you will select the horse you will ride."

Ordinarily, any young boy would be thrilled at the prospect, and, truthfully, Luis did feel a certain amount of excitement, but it was diminished by an overwhelming concern. How could he be a keeper of the Law of Moses and a teacher of its tenets while serving with his uncle? Turning to Don Luis, he placed a hand on his arm and with an attempt at enthusiasm, he exclaimed, "Uncle, I look forward to tomorrow. God bless us in our endeavors."

The governor gave him a resounding slap on the back. "You are an unusual boy, my nephew." Then, with a sweeping gesture, he bade them all goodnight.

The family talked late into the night about the implications and complications of this new development. Luis and Baltasar had become active in the community, seeking out 'conversos' willing to listen. The brothers were soon recognized as proselytizers and were sought out by many who wished to return to Judaism. With Luis leaving, the onus would be on Baltasar to continue the work, even though his father would assist.

Within the family, all were believers in the Mosaic Law except for the governor and Luis' oldest brother, Gaspar, who was a priest. For the most part, the family was cautious of Gaspar because his indoctrination and devotion to the Evangelical Law was intense. He had never known any other. Therefore, when they prayed together, they always concluded with "In the name of the Father, the Son and the Holy Ghost." Gaspar had always found this to be satisfactory behavior even though, secretly, he entertained some doubts about the family at times.

This particular Friday night, Gaspar had not joined the family. He had gone to the home of an Old Christian family to administer last rites to one of its members. His absence and the departure of the governor left the de Carvajals free to sing some hymns and recite prayers without restraints. Before they retired, led by Luis, they indulged in fervent recitations about the oneness of God and promised salvation by His Law.

The next day, carrying a doublet, denim breeches, boots, a breastplate and a harquebus, the governor returned to his sister's house. It was Saturday, the Sabbath, and Francisca and her daughter Isabel were observing the day of rest. As they sat chatting about Luis' impending departure, they heard the governor call from the doorway. They immediately grabbed some sewing — which they kept nearby for such exigencies — and by the time he entered the room, they looked as though they were mending garments. There could be no suspicion of any observance here.

Dona Francisca said, "Oh, Don Luis, you have come so early! Young Luis is on an errand — some business matter for his father. Will you wait, or shall I send him to you when he returns?"

The governor handed her the articles of clothing and accessories, which she placed on a chair nearby. The truth was that Luis had gone to the house of a "converso" where several neighbors were gathered for a prayer meeting which he would conduct.

"I believe I shall stay awhile and enjoy another glass of your wonderful brandy. Perhaps the boy will return soon." He settled into a nearby chair.

Dona Francisca and Isabel exchanged looks of frustration. They would have to continue the façade. She prayed he would not ask for something to eat. If he went into the kitchen, it would be obvious to him that the food prepared the night before was being kept warm on the stove. Hastening to the cupboard, she grabbed the bottle of brandy, quickly poured a drink, and offered it to her brother.

As Don Luis sat comfortably in an armchair, sipping his drink slowly, his sister observed him as he glanced around the sparse, simple furnishings and she wondered if he felt any pangs of guilt. This was not what he had promised them. She knew that his reputation as a governor was par excellence, but his level of awareness regarding his family's situation was minimal.

The governor looked fondly at his sister and niece, who were frantically sewing and making idle conversation. "When Luis comes home, we shall all pray together. This is a good day. He will officially become my aide-de-camp and a conquistador in the army of our King and Mother Church." As he tilted his head back and drained the last drops from his glass, he did not notice the vexation on the faces of the two women.

Suddenly the door flung open and an exuberant Luis came dashing across the room. He spotted his uncle at once and saw the look of chagrin on his mother's face. News of the prayer meeting and the new members who had joined them would have to wait. It was fortunate that he had not yelled out his usual "Good Sabbath" greeting as he came through the doorway.

"Uncle Luis, welcome! I ran home as quickly as I could in hopes of finding you here. Did you bring my uniform? Are we going to select my horse?"

The governor broke out into a lusty laugh. "Slow down, nephew. Yes, yes. Everything is here, and we shall select your horse tomorrow morning." Turning to Francisca, he said, "This is an amazing son you have here. He shall go far."

A knock on the door startled them. A soldier stood there asking to speak with the governor. Everyone but Don Luis felt instant terror. At the soldier's request, the governor excused himself and stepped outside. The family exchanged fearful glances. Had they been betrayed?

When Don Luis returned, he told them the sad news that Dona Guiomar, his wife, had died. An officer on an incoming ship had brought word of her demise. Although the family was saddened, they could not help a feeling of relief.

The scene that followed created pandemonium. Before she had embarked for New Spain, Isabel had promised Guiomar that she would attempt to convert Don Luis to the Old Religion. Hearing of Guiomar's death, Isabel felt that now was the moment to broach the subject since it was Guiomar's wish.

"Uncle Luis, I speak for your dear, departed Guiomar. You must stop following the Evangelical Law and turn to the Law of Moses instead. Only then will you be assured of salvation in the Hereafter."

The governor looked as if he had been struck by a thunderbolt. He slapped Isabel across the face and shouted, "I believe in Jesus Christ and have no desire to follow the religion of heretics. How dare you say you speak for my wife?"

His sister tried to calm him but he reviled her. "Your daughter is a demon and a disgrace to the de Carvajals. You would best see to it that she returns to the only true religion — to Jesus Christ and the Virgin Mary — and never blasphemes again!"

Isabel sat slumped in a corner of the room, sobbing violently. Luis tried to appease his uncle but the governor shrugged him off and continued his warning to his niece. "If you ever speak to me again about the Law of Moses, I shall kill you." To his sister he said, "This is one daughter you never should have given birth to."

Dona Francisca refrained from answering but her husband, angered, lashed out at Don Luis. "Do you really think you are an Old Christian? Your parents were secret worshippers of the Mosaic Law."

At this remark, the governor tore at his beard and cursed Don Francisco as a liar. "My family has always followed the Catholic faith. That is the only true faith. I am sick to death of Jews who preach stupidities." So saying, he stormed out of the house.

Now the possibility of being reported to the Inquisition rose like a specter before them. Would the governor, in his wrath, turn them in as secret worshippers? The decree of the Holy Office required that anyone suspected of "heretic" activities must be reported.

No one slept that night.

The next morning, a dour group sat around the kitchen table. The early hours had been spent asking God to spare them. They sat silently, eating. An unexpected Don Luis suddenly appeared at the door. He too looked gaunt and strained from not having slept. He entered the room, smiling weakly, with a persuasive argument upon his lips. "My family — I do not wish to change the plans we have made. We need each other. All night I deliberated and now I have a suggestion to make. If you will promise that you will give up your ridiculous observances and return to the true faith, I shall say nothing further about our little misunderstanding." He exacted promises from his sister, her husband and Isabel. He did not question Luis' loyalty. Had not the boy cried the night before when he heard the remarks made by his father and had sobbed, "How terrible!"

Their promises were a relief and Don Luis indicated that he considered the matter rectified. After a passionate lecture on the purity and goodness of Catholic doctrine, he turned to his nephew Luis. "Come, my dear lad, let us go to the stables and select a horse fine enough for a conquistador." He was the affable uncle once again.

In spite of the distress he had experienced the night before, Luis felt a sense of excitement and adventure. The wilderness, the natives, the unknown fascinated him. Perhaps it was even an opportunity to do God's work.

CHAPTER IV

ROAD TO TEMAPACHE

Although Luis had seen black people in Portugal, he was amazed at the large numbers he now saw in the small towns and mining areas through which he and his uncle led their contingent of men.

"Uncle, how did so many black people come to this land? Where did they come from?"

The governor explained, "These people were either bought or kidnapped from coastal regions of Africa and brought to New Spain on Spanish galleons to add to the work force. Much of the original native population was killed off, either by *conquistadores* or the disease which they brought to this land."

"I notice that although many work in the mines, many more work as household servants," Luis answered.

"That is true," agreed Don Luis. "Because they were acquired at a price, they are considered more valuable than the natives. Some freed blacks even served as conquistadores. It is sad that the original inhabitants of this land were decimated. With the proper treatment and conversion to the Catholic faith, things could have gone differently." Don Luis shook his head. "I have gotten into trouble with the viceroys because I advocate dealing fairly with the natives and the slaves. Anyway, when Spain witnessed Portugal's success in the slave trade, she soon followed suit."

"Was this long ago, Uncle?" Luis was curious.

"The first black slaves arrived in Hispaniola in 1502, and eventually slavery spread to the other colonies."

"Uncle, do you own any slaves?"

"My boy, I do not like to think that I 'own' another person. There are many who work for me on the plantations and in the mines. As an *encomendero*, I am responsible for their welfare. It is true that they must obey me and live according to certain regulations, but I believe in the fair treatment of these people. For that reason, I was successful in bringing peace and maintaining it in this territory."

"I am proud of you, Uncle." Luis could not help thinking, *It is unfortunate that you are not so liberal-minded about your family's beliefs.*

"My boy, you will do a fine job of helping me bring Christianity to these primitive people. We must do this to save their souls."

At that moment, Luis thought that silence was imperative.

As they made their way to Temapache, under the tutelage of his uncle Luis spent time learning how to determine the mineral wealth of an area and the tribute-paying capacity of each. Don Luis would need this information to estimate the distribution of *"encomiendas"* (land grants) to some of his conquistadores. While Luis was enthusiastic about learning these new things, he deplored the fact that he was expected to give instruction in Catholicism to the natives. He avoided this chore as much as possible, excusing himself for a variety of reasons to the friar who accompanied them.

The conquistadores of the sixteenth century were creatures of what had developed as a tradition: conquest. Gentlemen adventurers, for the most part, they were lured by gold and spurred by ambition, willing to leave their homelands for the unknown. Fearless, religious, and without conscience about familial responsibility, they fought the inhabitants and Mother Nature in the colonies of Spain. They captured; they conquered; they cavorted. Many a liaison was formed between soldier and native or black maiden. The progeny resulting from these partnerships were "mestivos" and "mulattoes".

During the ten year period he had spent away from Spain, the governor had had several affairs. Although he loved his wife dearly, it did not interfere with his carnal desires. Attractive, virile, and courageous, he commanded respect and admiration and the attention of females.

In the pacification of Temapache, he had developed a strong relationship with the 'cacique' of that village. The chief had offered him several maidens as gifts, but there was only one maiden who had stimulated the governor's interest and appetite — the favorite daughter of Chief Tlatlalu.

Pajara Blanca (White Dove), as Don Luis called her, was not only beautiful but also displayed a high degree of intelligence. In her tribe, she was a princess. The governor, who now had a decent command of the Mixtec language, spent a good part of his spare time with her, becoming more and more enthralled by her charm. Her father considered their relationship an honor, especially enjoying the obvious advantages of being in good favor with the governor.

Now, after many months and many stops along the way, the governor and his entourage continued north to Temapache. Don Luis thought about seeing his White Dove again. There was a stirring in his loins as he recalled their intimate moments. He remembered how awkward it had been at first. She was so young, only sixteen, and he had not wanted to frighten her. At her father's bidding, she had come, obediently, to the governor's quarters. When Don Luis saw her, his breath caught in his throat. She had been prepared as though for her wedding. Her hair was brushed to gleaming black satin and was adorned with an array of colored beads. She was clothed in a caftan, the fabric of which had been specially woven for such an occasion. The governor had been over-whelmed as she demurely entered the room and stood smiling at him. He had been speechless, so smitten by her beauty and graceful carriage. The intensity of his feelings had amazed him.

He had extended his hand to her, saying, "This will be a special night for my little princess."

She had smiled and lowered her gaze.

Don Luis had wooed her tenderly and skillfully. Their mutual emotional response had led to the consummation of their passion. White Dove told him later that she had been fearful, at first, because of stories she had heard from other maidens of the rough and insatiable sexual appetites of some soldiers. The act had been more like rape and the women had always felt abused and demeaned.

The governor had assured her, "My sweet one, you shall never feel that way with me. I shall cherish you and show you only kindness."

"I am grateful," she replied. "I shall return your kindness with my love, always."

Don Luis relished the thought of seeing her again. *It has been as long separation*, he thought. *I hope all is well with my Pajara Blanca.* He glanced sideways at his nephew and realized that he knew nothing about the boy's sexual experiences. *Well, I must speak with him about that. We much launch his career as a conquistador with a night of passion*, he promised himself.

They had been riding all day. The wooded terrain was difficult and the air was full of mosquitoes. Suddenly, they came to a clearing and found themselves facing a party of natives, plumed and painted, carrying bows and arrows. As one stepped forward, the governor's soldiers quickly raised their arquebuses, waiting for a signal. The contingent was comprised of new recruits who were not aware that the governor had made peace with these people and was welcome there. Luis was astonished when his uncle dismounted and shook hands with the scantily dressed, handsome brave who approached. He would soon learn just how much at home his uncle was in this strange territory of Nuevo Leon. After a brief, friendly conversation, the parties said farewell and moved on. They proceeded until they reached a large clearing where the governor gave orders to set up camp on the perimeter of what was obviously a small village. Adobes and small shacks were visible.

Within moments, they were approached by a tall, impressive, commanding figure of a man, accompanied by other natives, who exclaimed, "Ay, gobernador, it is good to see you. It has been too long."

"Yes, my friend. Let me introduce you to my nephew, who will someday be my heir."

They exchanged greetings and handshakes and then Don Luis excused himself to seek out his White Dove. Before he left, however, he issued orders to Luis. "You are in charge. May as well learn what leadership is all about, eh?" Without waiting for a protest from his nephew, he dashed off.

Later that evening, as they all sat banquet style at long tables, they enjoyed a feast of roasted meat and exotic, unique concoctions of herbs and vegetables, which were ravenously consumed by the hungry "*soldados*." Luis noticed that his uncle and the lovely daughter of the cacique often exchanged intimate glances and whispered remarks, after which she would giggle. Several times his uncle embraced her and kissed her with gusto, at which point, he would then wink broadly at his nephew.

The governor's men had not expected to fare this well in the wilderness. The temptation to come to this place had been the lust for silver and land. They had been promised great rewards. Anything else was a bonus. All this good food and beautiful women! They drank a hearty toast to the governor's health and saluted him. Don Luis was glad to see his men happy. He needed them to secure his position in the territory. A display of power helped to maintain control. These expeditions cost him plenty. Financing was his responsibility, so he had to make sure that these undertakings proved fruitful. The silver mines that he discovered and controlled were apportioned among his men and the "one-fifth" allotment to the Crown was set aside after he calculated his share to cover expenses.

When Luis was presented to the cacique as the governor's heir apparent, a big fuss was made over him and he was declared to be an "honorary cacique," as Don Luis was. The Chief was immediately presented with an impressive gift: a beautifully crafted sword of silver in a scabbard of the same precious metal. After they finished wining and dining, the sound of undulating rhythms was heard from drums. A line of lovely native girls came forward to dance the Dance of Peace and Harmony. Their half-naked bodies swaying and vibrating with the sensuous sounds stirred the emotions of the watchers — in many ways. Some of the men spontaneously jumped up, grabbed some of the girls, and tried to join in the dance. Everyone laughed.

When the dance was over, the Chief invited Luis to choose a maiden for his personal pleasure. Uncle Luis translated the invitation to his bright, loving nephew, whose eyes widened and jaw slackened. He fumbled for words. The governor exchanged some remarks with the Chief. His soldiers had a good laugh when Don Luis assessed the situation from the look on Luis' face. "*Dios mio* — the boy must still be a virgin! If he were not, he would be running off full speed with one of these pretties." When Don Luis explained this in Mixtec, the Chief and his men roared with laughter.

Luis, however, was mortified, but he pretended to enjoy the joke. Meanwhile, his innocent eyes glanced at the dancers and he could not help but wonder which one he should choose. The problem was quickly solved for him. His uncle playfully pulled one of the girls toward him and gently pushed her into his nephew's arms. "Now, my young lion — become a true conquistador. You must taste love as well as conquest. Go!"

The maiden laughed and took the "lion" by the hand and led him to an adobe close by.

Oh, Lord, thought Luis, *what would my beloved mother have to say about this?*

The next few weeks were busy ones for the governor and his nephew. For the latter, it was a learning experience through a hands-on relationship with the natives. Like his uncle, he was admired by their captives and accepted as an honorary brother. Because of his good looks and gallantry, Luis was the object of desire of every available female. Finally coming into his own, the new conquistador took full advantage of his situation. There were moments when he reflected upon his behavior and regretted his lack of devotion to his observance of the Law of Moses.

The governor had brought with them a friar whom he intended to leave with the natives to educate them and prepare them for conversion to the Catholic faith. Don Luis planned to build a church, place the friar in charge, and eventually baptize the Chief, his family, and the members of his tribe.

One day he asked Luis, "Nephew, are you spending a part of each day assisting the friar in expounding on the virtues of accepting our Lord Jesus Christ and the Blessed Mother Mary?"

Luis answered cautiously, "Of course, Uncle. I do so with much eagerness." He felt a churning in his stomach but remained cool and controlled.

"Good man," replied Don Luis.

Within a short time, Luis learned Mixtec and communicated fluently. His quick mind never ceased to amaze his uncle who well appreciated Luis' ability in ordering supplies for the troops and keeping records and accounts of the governor's mining operations. Don Luis praised him constantly. "You will be a fine leader and will govern my territories. Someday all my possessions will belong to you. You must remember to be fair and humane so that people will have trust in you. Above all, have faith in the Lord."

Luis, having no answer that his uncle would find suitable, merely nodded.

Within several months, the governor realized that Luis' supervisory duties were demanding most of his time and he was hard-pressed to maintain his bookkeeping. He solved the problem by sending for Baltasar. "You will keep all records and accounts," he told him, "so that your brother is free to supervise at the mines."

"It shall be done, Uncle," Baltasar assured him.

Neither Luis nor his brother was happy about the situation. This left only their father to continue the proselytizing and the support of the family.

When they had been in Temapache for a little over a year, a messenger brought the news that Don Francisco had become critically ill while on a business trip to Mexico City and was being cared for at a cousin's house. Because of the gravity of his condition, the family had requested that Luis be allowed to go to his father's bedside inasmuch as the family could not make the trip from Tampico.

Luis asked the governor for permission to go. "I regret that I must take this leave of absence but I must perform my duty to my dear father."

The governor reluctantly consented. "Yes, my boy. You must say goodbye and assure your father a good Christian burial. I cannot accompany you, so you will present my condolences to my brother-in-law."

"Of course, Uncle. I am sorry to leave you and I look forward to my return." Luis said these words with as much sincerity as he could muster.

Actually, he was anxious to see his father and spend some time in prayer with him and to fulfill his last wishes.

He bade his brother and uncle farewell. One of the soldiers familiar with the terrain escorted him to the road leading to Mexico City, at which point Luis continued on alone. After some hard riding, he arrived at his cousin's house. It grieved him to see the pitiable condition of his father. Don Francisco was dying. Luis could not believe it — his father was dying.

"Mi hijo," Francisco's eyes filled with tears at the sight of his beloved son. They hugged and both wept. He reached out his hand to Luis and told him, "There are certain things that you must do for me when I am called to God."

"Anything you want me to do, dear Father, I shall do," Luis assured him.

"I do not want to face my maker without being properly cleansed. Please see to it that my body is washed, and my nails and hair cut."

The significance of the request was not lost on the son. Luis fully understood the preparation for burial according to Jewish ritual.

Just before he expired, Don Francisco asked for a priest's last rites and advised his son, "Now, Luis, go to church so that Father Antonio may hear your confession." Again, the significance was clear: the outward observance of necessity as opposed to the observance of the heart.

After funeral arrangements and interment took place, Luis decided to pay his mother a brief visit. It meant more time and travel, but he wanted to tell her himself that his father had been buried in accordance with Jewish ritual and that his pallbearers had all been Secret Jews. They carried Don Francisco to his resting place — in the Dominican Monastery in Mexico City!

CHAPTER V

THE WEDDINGS

Luis had another matter of importance to discuss with his mother. It involved an opportunity for marriage for Leonor and Catalina, two of his sisters. During his stay in Mexico City, while tending to his father, he was approached by Antonio Diaz de Caceres and Jorge de Almeida, wealthy New Christians, with offers to marry the girls. These men were friends of Don Francisco. They were of high station and, best of all, Secret Jews. Luis was positive that his mother would accept these suitors gladly. For some time, the governor had been trying to find husbands from Old Christian families for his nieces. Francisco and Francisca had forestalled any such possibility at every turn. It was clear that Don Luis had a vested interest in arranging such marriages. Marrying Old Christians would eradicate any inclination in the girls to practice Judaism. Such alliances would strengthen the governor's position as an Old Christian, should his lineage ever come into question.

As Luis made his way to his mother's house, he was painfully aware of the poor condition of the area. Homes were nothing more than hovels. The air was dank and moist and the atmosphere was dismal and depressing. *Well,* he thought, *the news I bring will change all that. My mother and siblings shall enjoy a better life if the suitors are true to their promises.*

There was much happiness in the house upon his arrival. His mother was overjoyed to see her son again after such a long interval. She could not stop hugging and kissing him and thanking the Lord for this wonderful blessing. Finally, they spoke of Don Francisco.

"What of your padre? Tell me everything." Tears glistened in Francisca's eyes.

With great sorrow, Luis told her of how he had stayed at his cousin's house for several months. "I did the best that I could to help Father but his illness was too formidable. We had a long talk and do not worry, Mother — he was buried as a Jew." He assured her that all outward precautions had been taken to avoid any suspicion. "Mother," he winked at her, "we buried him in good Christian ground."

"Well done, my son. I am at peace with what you have told me. I knew that if your father did not survive, you would be sure to tell me yourself. You are a fine son and I am proud of you."

They spent some time talking about Don Francisco's last days. Luis told her of the many friends who had visited and of the theological discussions they had. "Mother, there are so many of us here. The more I travel around, the more I become aware of the work that has to be done to restore our people to the Mosaic Law."

Dona Francisca asked, "How will you do this if you must serve with your uncle?"

"I shall find a way. God will provide," he answered. Then he broached the subject of the marriage proposals.

The family had been in the Panuco area since their arrival in 1580. Instead of improving, things had gotten steadily worse. The governor contributed very little to their sustenance; in fact, he had, literally, left them to their own devices. With Don Francisco gone and both Luis and Baltasar in the service of the governor, the family was barely above the poverty level.

Luis' visit and the news of the proposals gave them new hope. From the moment that Dona Francisca had acquiesced to the marriages, days were spent in speculation and prayer. She wondered if and how their lives would change. From Luis' description of the prospective grooms, prospects looked good. Still, she was afraid to get her hopes up too high.

Antonio Diaz de Caceres and Jorge de Almeida were two of the wealthiest New Christians in Mexico. Antonio was the older by ten years, being forty-six years old, and the more handsome of the two. In his youth, he had achieved status in the Royal Court of Portugal and had served in Portugese armadas. His first marriage, at the age of 24, had sadly ended with the death of his wife and child. Most of his time was spent in traveling to the Orient to secure items for resale in New Spain and for export to Europe.

Jorge de Almeida, heavy set with a chestnut colored beard, was not a physically attractive man; however, he was a talented entrepreneur who owned silver mines in Taxco and also processing plants for the precious metal. Importing and exporting provided him with a lucrative source of income. His reputation as a businessman was impeccable and, on many occasions, he had served as purchasing agent for the Crown.

Both men had been friends of Don Francisco and at his demise were much concerned about his wife and siblings. They had, on occasion, seen

Catalina — not yet in her teens — and Leonor — just out of them. They had approached Luis to help the family in its dire circumstances and, also, because they believed it was time to marry.

First Antonio had asked, "What will your family do now, my boy? Your poor mother and brothers and sisters! We know how hard you and Baltasar have tried to support them."

"We shall manage as well as we can," answered Luis. "Our faith in God shall sustain us and our fortunes shall change, I am certain."

At this point, Jorge, anxious to broach the subject of marriage, sputtered out, "We would like to marry your sisters, Leonor and Catalina. What do you think?" His brash outburst embarrassed him and he smiled sheepishly. Antonio shot him a glance that would have melted armor. Tact was not Jorge's forte.

Antonio apologetically intervened. "Son, Jorge spoke so quickly. I hope you are not offended. I had intended to negotiate the matter with more finesse but, the truth is, we would appreciate it if you would present our proposals to your dear mother."

Inwardly, Luis was overjoyed. This unexpected turn of events presented tremendous possibilities for the family. If nothing else, certainly its economic and social conditions would improve. "I shall be happy to discuss the matter with my mother whom I intend to visit when I leave Mexico City," he assured them. He did not wish to appear too anxious. A good negotiator does not show his hand.

Antonio and Jorge, excited with anticipation, alternated with assurances of their capabilities to support the girls in style. Antonio said, "They shall want for nothing. We are successful businessmen and world traders."

"And we shall provide a fine home and adorn your sisters with jewels and beautiful garments," added Jorge.

Antonio promised, "Your family shall prosper from our marriages."

After some further discussion, they shook hands. "You shall have your answer shortly," Luis told them.

As soon as Antonio and Jorge received word by messenger of Dona Francisca's approval, they immediately set about to arrange for the dowries they had agreed to provide. Within a short period of time, gifts began arriving at the de Carvajal residence. The girls squealed with joy as they opened their presents. Not only were there casks of delicious jellies, cheeses, delicate cakes and wine, but also beautiful garments of silk and velvet with matching dainty slippers. A far cry from the torn skirts and mended shirtwaists! The girls hugged each other, jumping up and down and dancing about as they unpacked one box after another.

Dona Francisca laughingly admonished, "You will expire before you can wear anything if you do not stop screaming and jumping so." Francisca had to contain herself as well. When she opened her gifts and those of her other children, she gushed, "Such generosity! I have never seen anything like it."

Luis' reunion with his mother and siblings was short-lived. A few days after his arrival, a column of soldiers was dispatched from Temapeche to relieve those on duty in Tampico. They brought with them orders from the governor who was on the move to San Gregorio. After a few days of rest and relaxation, the Tampico regiment, with Luis in command, was to rejoin the governor.

Dona Francisca confided to her son, "Listen, Luis, your uncle is to know nothing of the forthcoming marriages. Remember how hard he tried to find Old Christian suitors for your sisters?"

"Yes, Mother. I am aware that this will anger him, so I shall say nothing." He knew that his mother feared it might spur the governor to vengeance. She often felt that her brother entertained thoughts of reporting the family as Judaizers because, at times, he displayed a suspicious nature.

Luis was busy for days rounding up provisions for the trip and planning the route he would take to San Gregorio. Finally, all was in readiness and, after a tearful departure, he led his soldiers out. His loved ones watched as he mounted his horse and issued orders. *How handsome my son is*, thought Francisca. *A true leader, fearless and strong.*

He did make quite a picture with his silver helmet gleaming in the sunlight, covering his ebony hair and framing his alabaster face. The rest of his costume was impressive as well, from his mail breastplate down to his silver-ornamented boots. As he raised his right arm to signal his men forward, he turned and flashed a dazzling smile at his family. Francisca watched until the last signs of the troops disappeared from view. She walked slowly back to the house with a prayer on her lips that the good Lord would watch over her son.

The little town of Tampico did not remain quiet for long. One afternoon, suddenly, it was buzzing with excitement at the arrival of an impressive entourage. A neighbor, Maria, knocked loudly on the de Carvajal's door, imploring, "Come quickly, Francisca — there are two finely dressed gentlemen approaching with their servants and they are asking for you." Maria could scarcely contain herself. "Hurry!" she shouted.

Isabel got to the door first. "What is going on? Who asks for us, Maria?"

"Oh, Isabel, two fine gentlemen on horseback...I have never seen such splendor...but come, see for yourself! They are here." Maria fluttered like a frantic butterfly. Isabel laughed and playfully pushed her aside. It was her turn now to stare in disbelief.

There on splendid steeds sat Antonio and Jorge, outfitted in velvet and leather with gold medallions hanging from their necks, their heads covered with stylishly plumed hats. Accompanying them were several servants tending to many chests and luggage. The extravagance of the scene was overwhelming.

Isabel, speechless but only for a moment, ran back into the house screaming for her mother and sisters. "Madre, Leonor, Catalina! Come quickly! The grooms have arrived! They are right outside the house!"

Leonor and Catalina were in a dither. It was all Francisca could do to calm them and herself. "If you do not stop giggling, Leonor, I shall stuff a handkerchief in your mouth and, you, Catalina, deport yourself in a ladylike manner. Even if your sister is silly, you are old enough to know better." The anxious Mother wanted nothing to dissuade the potential grooms. Obediently, the girls followed her out to greet Antonio and Jorge and make them welcome.

The first to dismount, Antonio removed his hat with a flourish and approached Francisca. Taking her hand in his, he slowly lifted it to his lips. "Senora de Carvajal, allow me to introduce myself. I am Antonio Diaz de Caceres, and I come with my friend, Jorge de Almeida, to make arrangements for our marriages to your lovely daughters, Leonor and Catalina."

Dona Francisca smiled broadly. "Welcome, *senores*. We are happy to see you." Noticing her daughters standing like two statues, she nudged each one forward whereupon they recovered sufficiently to stammer a "Welcome to you both. We are pleased to meet you at last."

Tall and handsome Antonio was no stranger to gallantry. He quickly took the right hand of each girl and lightly kissed each in turn. This evoked giggles again from the brides-to-be, but a warning flash from their mother's eyes brought them to an abrupt end.

Jorge then followed Antonio's example. There were more polite exchanges and then the servants were ordered to bring the trunks and baggage into the house.

The other de Carvajal siblings — ten-year old Miguel, six-year old Anica and fourteen-year old Mariana were summoned from their rooms. They had been peeking out the windows all the time and, when Francisca called to them, they raced down the stairs, hardly containing their excitement.

The servants unwrapped one fine object after another: more silk and velvet finery, silver trimmed slippers, purses of fine leather, jewelry and jewelry boxes that dazzled, small tables of inlaid mahogany...the array seemed endless. This was far beyond anything the family had ever hoped or prayed for and they could hardly contain the "ohs" and "ah+0s" that escaped their lips.

Antonio pulled Dona Francisca aside. "Come, Mother — let us drink a toast to the health and happiness of all present and to the happy days ahead."

"*Seguramente.* Thank you, senor."

One of the servants was a tall, muscular Negro whom Antonio had saved from the slave market by taking him personally under his wing — Nazareo, by name. He and, later, his wife Emilia were brought to the de Caceres house. They were totally devoted to Antonio.

"Nazareo, open some bottles of wine," Antonio ordered. He turned to the others. "Let us drink to a new life."

Mariana ran to get some glasses. Bottles were opened and poured and everyone, even little Miguel and Anica, toasted the couples. Jorge lifted his glass. "To good health, to life, to happiness. May the Almighty cause His countenance to shine upon us." All echoed his sentiments with a hearty "Amen!"

The grooms, true to their word, gave Francisca several thousand pesos for the dowries they had promised her. She found it difficult to control her emotions as she kissed each of them and thanked them profusely.

"Now to set the date, Mother. What is your pleasure?" Jorge was eager.

"I would be most pleased if the weddings took place in March, at the time of the Passover celebration," she answered.

"So be it," Antonio confirmed and filled the glasses once again.

A day after the departure of Antonio and Jorge, Francisca's oldest son Gaspar, the priest, arrived for a brief visit. He was amazed at what he saw in the house and when he learned of the imminent marriages, he exclaimed, "Wonderful! I shall come back to solemnize the ceremonies."

No one uttered a word against the suggestion. *In fact*, thought Francisca, *what could be more appropriate — and safe?*

Gaspar's presence in the house was both blessing and burden. As always, it provided a deterrent to any suspicions about the family's religious activities, but it also imposed restrictions upon the family's behavior. The least concerned was Isabel. She observed fasting days when she so wanted and refrained from doing any chores on Saturday until after sundown. Gaspar took note of her actions as his doubts and frustrations mounted. Finally, one day when he observed her fasting, he angrily accused her. "Sister, I do not see you praying at the altar in the prayer room or saying your rosary. Your actions — these fasts — reflect more upon the Old Bible rituals than those of our Holy Church. I suggest you pay more attention to your behavior."

Alert to the danger, Isabel meekly agreed. "You are my brother and a priest and you know what is best for me. I shall do as you say."

"Yes," he admonished, sternly, "and save your housework for a day other than the Lord's Day."

Isabel did not pursue the issue any further. She merely nodded.

A look of agitation flickered across Gaspar's face. He opened his mouth as though to speak but harumphed instead and quickly strode out of the house.

CHAPTER VI

CHANGING OF THE GUARD

After Luis and his contingent departed from Tampico, the newly arrived troops remained under the command of a lieutenant until the arrival of the dashing Captain Felipe Nunez, who was one of Governor de Carvajal's highest ranking officers. The captain's orders included not only the protection of the town from the warlike Chichimec Indians, but also the establishment of Padre Delgado as the village priest. It was the governor who had financed the building of the crude little church in the center of town and now, more than ever, he was anxious that the villagers remain faithful and abiding followers of the Church.

His particular concern stemmed from the King's appointment of a new viceroy to Nuevo Leon. Memories of his conflict with Don Alvaro Monrique de Zuniga concerning the boundaries of his territory were still fresh in his mind. Don Luis suspected that it would not be long before there would be a rise in the activities of the Holy Office, inasmuch as viceroys were an arm of the Church and their job was to ferret out "heretics" and "enemies" of the Evangelical Law.

Once again, the suspicions about the family's behavior came to haunt him and caused him sleepless nights. When he assigned Captain Nunez to Tampico, he made sure that his duties included a grand display for the Church. He ordered the captain, "You will install Father Delgado as the leader of the flock in the Church of the Resurrection. Make sure you hold impressive festivities in the village square. Give the people refreshments and provide some music. They will be grateful and happy for the celebration."

Captain Nunez clicked his heels and saluted. "I shall see to all the details, according to your orders, Sir."

"And, too," the governor continued," you will present yourself to my sister, Dona Francisca de Carvajal and her children. When you do, give her this message: tell her that her brother prays for their well-being everyday and is content in the thought that they are living as good Christians."

The captain found the latter part of the statement a bit puzzling but did not question it.

Upon his arrival in Tampico, he set about to carry out the governor's instructions. Arrangements were made for the padre's celebration and announcements were posted around the town square for all to see. In this miserable place, the news of a *fiesta* brought joy to its inhabitants, whether or not they cared about the reason for it.

On the Sunday following Felipe's arrival, a special mass was held at the little church in which the vicar was installed at a salary of two thousand pesos. Later, everyone took to the streets where tables were set up with a variety of foods and beverages. Musicians strummed familiar tunes on their guitars and the villagers sang along, with gusto. They wined, dined, and danced in a somewhat frenzied attempt to convince themselves that all was well.

Three days later, Felipe paid a formal visit to introduce himself to the de Carvajals. When he repeated the governor's precise words, a chill of foreboding swept over the family. Isabel and her mother exchanged glances but betrayed nothing of their inner turmoil. Evasively, Francisca answered, "Thank you, Captain, for your kind message. We are happy to hear from my dear brother and hope he is in good health."

Felipe assured them of this. During the course of the afternoon, he became more and more aware of how attractive Isabel was. When he was about to take his leave, he promised, "I shall see you all again very soon, if you will permit me. The governor has asked me to look to your needs."

Francisca thought, *Such sudden concern for us. There must be a reason.* At that moment, in a good frame of mind, she attributed only the best of motives to him. She smiled and thanked the captain.

Isabel demurely lowered her glance and said coquettishly, "Oh, *Senor*, it will be a pleasure to see you again. Please stop by soon." She blushed at her own aggressiveness. Felipe's handsome face and excellent physique awakened a passion within Isabel that she thought was buried with her beloved husband.

Felipe flashed her a disarming smile, saluted gallantly, and bade them all a pleasant good evening. "I shall return shortly," he promised. He, too, could not ignore the stirrings within him. *Perhaps Tampico would not be a dull assignment after all*, he mused.

When they were sure that he had departed, each blurted out comments filled with curiosity and hope. It seemed that their luck continued to improve dramatically. Francisca gushed, "First the betrothals of Leonor and Catalina, and now a handsome officer to cater to our needs, courtesy of dear Uncle Luis. *Gracias Dios! Gracias el Senor.* Our prayers have been answered." She clasped her hands together and closed her eyes momentarily, then she laughed and hugged them all.

Isabel had been consumed with desire immediately. A widow for many years, she had remained faithful to her deceased husband. Now she was amazed and, yes, shocked at the thoughts besieging her mind. All this was not lost on her mother, who would be happy to see her daughter with love again in her life. However, she was fully aware that the man would have to be a follower of the Mosaic Law because Isabel was devoted to the practices of Judaism. For some reason, Francisca felt uneasy about Felipe and sensed a need for caution. Isabel, on the other hand, had already established in her mind that Felipe was probably a Secret Jew. Even though she had no knowledge of this fact, wishing made it so.

The captain paid another visit two days later. This time he brought with him gifts of imported delicacies: coffee, tea, jars of honey, jellies, pipes of wine, and three, live, local chickens. Francisca was grateful that she would be able to butcher the fowl herself, according to ritual. She did not reveal this to Felipe, however. She called to her servant to put the chickens in a pen in back of the house.

"*Muchos gracias, Senor.* This is so kind of you," gushed Isabel. "Will you join us? We were just about to have our midday meal."

"I would be most honored, *Senora,*" Felipe accepted. He took the seat offered him at the table. "You have wonderful children, Dona Francisca," he continued. He took inventory of Leonor, Catalina, Mariana, Miguel, Anica, and Isabel. *Luscious Isabel,* he thought. "I look forward to meeting Gaspar, your oldest son. I already have had the pleasure of serving with Luis and Baltasar — fine young men. Luis is a remarkable lad. He will go far," and then he quickly added, "as will Baltasar, I am sure."

"Thank you for your kind words," the proud mother answered.

When the food was served and wine poured, Felipe lifted his glass. "To health, to good fortune," he toasted the gathering. As he looked around, his gaze briefly rested upon Isabel, whose radiant face sent out a message of sweet surrender.

The dog days of summer wore on and Felipe assumed the role of mentor and protector of the de Carvajals. From time to time, soldiers would come and go from the governor's expedition, bearing messages and inquiring about the family. The captain's answers always confirmed that all was well. He described the pleasant hours spent with the family and how they attended church together on Sundays. Unaware of the family's secret regarding the imminent marriages, in one of his communiques he wrote about the happy preparations for the weddings of Leonor and Catalina.

At first, the captain had limited his courtship of Isabel to visits with the family. Finally, one evening after dinner, he asked if Isabel might enjoy going for a stroll along the banks of the Panuco.

"Oh, yes," she impulsively responded. Trying hard not to betray her enthusiasm, she rose slowly from her chair, stammering, "I shall get my shawl. It is often damp by the river in the evening."

Dona Francisca watched her flustered daughter and would have laughed had she not thought it would embarrass her. Instead, she said, "Go, my dears. Enjoy the evening."

As the couple strolled along the banks of the river, now and then they touched — a thigh brushing against a thigh, a steadying hand on an arm. The rocky terrain caused them to walk with an uneven gait and, every few moments, Felipe held Isabel firmly around the waist as he helped her over some slippery spots. The day had slowly drawn to a close and light was waning rapidly. Soon the beautiful hues of dusk colored the sky.

"Perhaps we should return," suggested Isabel.

Felipe stopped abruptly and, placing both hands on her shoulders, turned her to him. He did not say a word but just stood there, looking deeply into her eyes. Slowly, he cupped her face in his hands. Isabel was sure he could hear the sound of her accelerated heartbeats. She was overwhelmed.

Ever ready with a talent for the right gestures, Felipe gently touched her hair and placed his lips lightly upon hers, looking at her longingly as he swept her into his arms. Isabel closed her eyes, feeling she might faint. Felipe brushed his lips across her eyelids, kissed the tip of her nose, and then passionately possessed her mouth. She uttered a little cry as she returned his fervor.

Felipe broke the silence. "My love, we must follow our hearts. When will you come to me?"

She mustered enough voice to whisper, "Whenever you will have me, Senor."

"What better time than now, my sweet?" he softly cajoled.

Isabel barely had time to take notice of his small but clean quarters. Felipe lit several candles and, as they fluttered, they cast shadows that danced and skipped along the walls. In spite of its rustic setting, to Isabel it was the most romantic place in the whole world. The attentive captain quickly poured some wine and toasted, "To Isabel, the loveliest flower in Tampico and the love of my life."

A tear, like a drop of quicksilver, glided down her cheek as she responded, "To my hero, my new-found love."

In the warm glow of the candlelight, they stood looking at each other, absorbing the intimacy of the moment. Then Felipe removed her shawl and set it aside. Her breasts heaved and she inhaled deeply. He slowly unbuttoned her blouse as he kissed her ears, her neck, her bosom. Isabel felt complete abandonment as he led her to his bed where he undressed her and then gently covered her with a light blanket while he, with great haste, removed his uniform and undergarments. As he lay beside her, he cradled her in his arms and softly sang an old Spanish love song. He spoke to her in endearing terms as he caressed her body. Isabel was amazed at how at ease she was and she responded with a passion she had long forgotten.

Felipe kissed every part of her body until she begged him to consummate their act of love. "My love, take, me possess me. I want to give myself completely to you."

Rising to the occasion, he created a memorable moment in the history of seduction. His lovemaking was that of a master craftsman. He even surprised himself at his ability to prolong "the ultimate". Now, sensing that he should wait no longer, he entered her slowly.

As they lay there, spent and barely able to say a word, Isabel felt such happiness and contentment. She thought, *I shall offer a prayer of gratitude to the Lord as soon as I get home.* Her thoughts were interrupted by a persistent Felipe who pulled her to him and kissed her demandingly. Isabel's body responded immediately and her mind was not too far behind.

When Isabel returned home later that night, her mother looked at her face and surmised that the "taking" of Isabel had been a mutual triumph. Francisca waited to see if her daughter would volunteer any information, but all she got was a fleeting view of her back as she disappeared up the stairs.

Once in her room, joyful Isabel, grateful Isabel thanked God for the blessings He had bestowed upon her. "Next time, I shall ask Felipe to pray with me," she vowed aloud.

When the governor received Felipe's message about the intended weddings, it was as though an explosion had gone off in his face. What? His nieces getting married and he was not told by the family? He could barely contain his outrage and immediately sent for his nephew. Luis stood before his apoplectic uncle within minutes.

"What sort of tyranny is this? You must have known your sisters were betrothed when you returned to camp. How could you not tell me? Am I not the benefactor of this family?"

Benefactor, indeed, thought Luis derisively. Instead, he said, "Uncle, it all happened so fast, we thought we would surprise you with the good news when the preparations were in place. I regret that you did not hear it from me first. But, be happy! Your sister and the family will be well-cared for." *As opposed to your stinginess and neglect, you old reprobate*, thought Luis.

By the time this conversation took place, the marriages were a fait accompli, safe from any interference by Don Luis. He asked his nephew, "Are these grooms from good Christian families?" This was his main concern.

"Have no fear, Uncle. They are devout New Christians, successful businessmen from respected families."

The governor breathed a sigh of relief. He would have preferred men from Old Christian stock but if they are devout New Christians, that would put an end to his nieces' clandestine practices of Jewish rituals. "Come, dear nephew — let us pray together for the happiness of your darling sisters."

They knelt. Luis chanted, in Latin, the closest prayer befitting the circumstances. With eyes closed, his uncle directed his passion to the Lord Jesus Christ. He was not aware that Luis did not make the sign of the cross when his prayer ended. What disturbed him was that he did not recall hearing the name of the Savior mentioned. However, there was no time for questions for at that exact moment Baltasar was hastening toward them with an official-looking document bearing the seal of the Office of the Viceroy.

CHAPTER VII

TROUBLED WATERS

Before Viceroy Zuniga left Spain for the New World, he and King Charles discussed the role of the conquistadors. Zuniga told him, "There is no doubt, Your Majesty, that some of these men have become too powerful. They are *encomenderos* of large portions of land, title to which should belong directly to the Crown."

"That is a plausible concept and one long maintained by the throne and the viceroys," responded the King, "but these conquistadores were brave enough to lead expeditions in the face of great and unknown dangers — and at their own expense. Remember, they have many loyal followers."

"True, Sire, but the ultimate control must rest with the throne," Zuniga persisted. "Your viceroys should be in control of the administration of these conquests. Men like Governor de Carvajal, for instance, should not exert power and influence to a higher degree than that of the Royal House. He and the others must know that they answer to the throne through its representative, the Office of the Viceroy."

"We have pursued this course for many years," the king replied, "and it has not been a judicious one. In fact, it presents many problems. After all, we did promise these men that not only do they own these lands, but it may be willed to their heirs, as well."

"But, your majesty, control is of the utmost importance in New Spain. I beg you to allow me to pursue the course I proposed to you. It will assure the position of the Spanish realm in the New World." Zuniga waited for a reply.

After some moments, King Charles said, "Make your arrangements accordingly. But I warn you, be sure you offer just cause for deposing any conquistador, especially one with the power and popularity of a de Carvajal."

Zunigo did not display the joy he felt. This was exactly the instruction he wanted. "Your will shall be done for God, for country," he promised. To himself, he mused, *Now Don Luis de Carvajal — we shall see just how impenetrable you are.*

Viceroy Zuniga arrived in Mexico with a specific agenda and a determination to see it through. His main objective was to "dethrone" Governor de

Carvajal and take control of his territories in the name of the King. Zuniga was like a man possessed. To the governor's credit, the viceroy had never been able to find a weak chink in his armor. He enjoyed a reputation for honesty and efficient administration. Even the Mexican courts had upheld his claim to his land. Yet, Zuniga persisted, there must be some weakness, some fallibility. *Every man has one and I shall find his*, he promised himself.

Don Luis was not in good spirits. He was not happy that the family had kept the weddings a secret, nor was he happy about the suspicions which plagued him about their religious bent. These factors inflamed the harassment he was now suffering since the delivery of the documents from Viceroy Zuniga, who seemed determined to confront him at every opportunity. Don Luis dreaded to think of the attacks he would suffer if the viceroy were to delve into his family's activities. If he were to find even a shred of evidence that could link him to a Jewish heritage...The governor winced.

His dark mood eventually brought about a rift between him and his nephew, Luis. During one of their conversations, the uncle commented, "I do not see you attending any of the services at the church, nor are you involved in educating the natives in the practices of Catholicism."

Luis quickly defended himself. "Uncle, I am so busy attending to the needs of the encampment and also supervising the workers at your silver mines that I have no time, unfortunately, to join you in church activities." He hoped this would assuage his uncle's wrath. It did not.

"Nephew, I do not believe you to be a true Catholic. Your actions disturb me." Don Luis was shouting now. "Devotion to the Lord is necessary every day!"

Cautiously, the boy parried, "Uncle, I do not understand your anger. I have tried to do all you have asked."

"Yes, in all fairness, you have served me well as a conquistador and managed my business affairs. But you fool me not, nephew. Your soul is tainted. You cling to dead beliefs." In a rage, he continued to spew accusations at the startled youth. "Your mother and her children have turned away from the only true God. They are all 'blind'! For a long time now, I have found their behavior suspect but I never dreamed that you would betray me."

"Uncle, my mother and siblings — all of us — live as good Christians."

"So? Then why was your father prepared for burial according to Jewish rituals?" He spat the words out. Luis could not help but react.

"Ah ha — you show surprise that I am aware of what happened. I said nothing because you know that I would have to report the family to the Holy

Office. Now I am not sure that I should not have done so."

Luis recoiled in horror. "Uncle, I do not understand..." He was cut short with an ominous warning.

"Stop, Luis — do not give me more cause to disown you. Your brother Gaspar, the priest, told me about his observations of the goings-on in the family."

Startled, Luis could only stare at him. He saw not only an angry man but a frightened one. *There is more to this than meets the eye*, he thought. *My uncle is in trouble, no doubt something to do with the problems since the viceroy's arrival.* From earlier conversations with Don Luis, he gathered that Zuniga had a vendetta against Don Luis which concerned itself with his being made Governor of Nuevo Leon and his attitude of fair treatment of the natives and slaves.

Fear closed tight fingers around Luis' heart. It was time to return to his mother, to see to the safety of his family. His instincts warned him that dire days lay ahead and that his uncle would be of no help. The next words he heard reinforced his decision to leave.

"Nephew, this is a sorry turn of events. If the Office of the Viceroy connects me in any way with Judaizers, I am a dead man."

Luis tried to calm him. "You have a fine reputation and live your life as a devout Christian. Do not concern yourself."

The governor exploded. "That is exactly the point! And I have ruined everything by bringing you and your wretched family here. It will prove my downfall. I see now that I must break all ties." His anger accelerated. "And you! You are my biggest disappointment, not worthy of my name and title."

Luis sensed he must leave as soon as possible. "Uncle, my brother Baltasar and I shall leave at once. It is obvious you no longer want us here."

"And good riddance to that traitor, too," muttered the distraught man.

"I wish you well, Uncle." Luis tried to embrace him but met with stiff resistance. "Adios, Tio." Luis walked away slowly, mounted his horse, and went in search of his brother.

After the weddings, Antonio and Jorge moved their brides, together with Francisca, Mariana and Anica into two large houses in Mexico City. Miguel, under Isabel's supervision, remained in school in Tampico. Mexico City opened up a whole new world for them and they enjoyed all the comforts their husbands' wealth could provide.

Isabel chose to remain in Tampico because she and the family assumed her relationship with Felipe was one of commitment. When Luis and Baltasar returned to the town, they were surprised to find their sister and Miguel still there and the family now in Mexico City. Isabel told them all the news and, in glowing terms, she described her new-found love and their relationship. The name Felipe Nunez tickled Luis' memory.

Isabel happily explained, "I shall stay here as long as Felipe is assigned to this area. When that changes, we shall make our plans accordingly."

At first, the brothers were glad for her. Luis observed, "You have been a widow and without a man for so long, my beautiful sister. It is time for you to love again. When may we meet your wonderful captain?"

Baltasar quipped good-naturedly, "Soon we shall be going to a wedding, eh?"

Isabel playfully slapped him on the shoulder and blushed. "I shall make dinner for all of us tomorrow night and you shall meet my handsome Felipe."

Luis said, "*Bueno*. It shall be a pleasure." The brothers kissed her and wished her well.

The next day, Luis and Baltasar went about renewing friendships and business contacts and reestablishing themselves in the community. This was not a problem. Well-known and well-liked, they were welcomed with open arms. Their activities would take them mainly to Mexico City where they would be in close proximity to the family.

Later that evening when they were bathing and dressing to go to dinner at their sister's house, Luis suddenly asked his brother, "Baltasar, do you remember a Captain Nunez from our expeditions to Taxco? A handsome fellow, as I recall, who spent most of the time abusing the male natives, and putting his hands on and under the garments of any maiden who crossed his path?"

Baltasar's first reaction was a loud, spontaneous laugh which quickly faded into a low, hoarse whisper. "Is it possible? Oh, God, please let it not be so! Poor Isabel."

Luis continued. "In fact, the governor had warned the captain about his cruelties and womanizing. Remember how the ambitious Nunez became so cautious about his behavior, going out of his way to endear himself to Uncle Luis. He even attended church with him." He pondered a moment. "What plans does this conquistador have for himself and — more importantly — for our sister?"

Ever the optimist, Baltasar offered, "Perhaps this is not the same man. Nunez is a common name."

"True," replied Luis, not believing it for one moment.

At dinner that night, the brothers' worst fears were confirmed. There he sat, beaming at them and toasting to their good health, the one and the same Captain Nunez. "It is good to see you again, my lads. Let us drink to our reunion."

He is an idiot, thought Luis. *Does he really believe that we are not aware of what a scoundrel he is?* Luis' heart broke as he watched how oblivious and ecstatic Isabel was. *Should he betray Nunez? Perhaps he is a changed man. Who knows? Look how radiant my lovely sister is. How can I hurt her?*

Baltasar looked to Luis for some indication as to how to proceed. Luis raised his glass of wine and proposed a toast. "Let us drink to true love and happiness and to our beautiful sister whom we shall watch over and protect always." Echoing these sentiments looking directly at Captain Nunez, Baltasar smiled and thought, *Only a fool would take that toast lightly.*

With tears in her eyes, Isabel ran to her brothers and kissed each on the cheek. The good captain, already sure of his place in the family, nodded enthusiastically. He knew nothing of the rift that had occurred between the governor and his nephews, nor did he realize that the Holy Office was interested in the genealogy of Governor Luis de Carvajal y de la Cueva.

It had never occurred to Isabel that Felipe was not a follower of the religion she held so dearly and clung to so steadfastly. She was careful, nevertheless. She wanted to hear it from his own lips. *Perhaps*, she wondered, *he was not sure of her*. It was time to ask some revealing questions, she decided, so that they may declare themselves.

One evening, as they enjoyed dinner together and sipped the fine wine Felipe provided, Isabel, a little loose of tongue, asked, "*Caro mio*, do you not agree that the coming of the Messiah will bring deliverance to all who have kept the faith?"

Felipe, a little more than slightly intoxicated, sobered at once and lashed out at her. "What are you saying, you foolish woman? Christ is the Messiah. I believe in Him and I shall die in that belief."

A shocked Isabel, tears flooding, retorted, "You are wrong, my love. The Messiah has yet to come and when he does, he will save us all. The God of the Law of Moses is the only true God."

She recoiled in terror at Felipe's next words. "If it were not for my concern for your uncle, the governor, I would report you and your family to the Inquisition."

Isabel could not believe what she was hearing. How could she have been duped for so long? She must say something to diffuse the potential danger. Coyly, she admonished him. "My love, I was only testing the strength of your faith. I am happy that you are so steadfast and resolute." She reached her arms out to him to embrace him but he flung her aside. In a moment, the door slammed shut behind him.

Fear gripped Isabel and anguish brought a flood of tears. How could she have been so mistaken? She must warn her brothers before they leave for Mexico City. The family was in jeopardy.

When Felipe stormed out of the house, he decided it was time to rejoin the governor who would find his news most interesting and, to be sure, disturbing. Felipe said nothing to anyone and refrained from reporting anything to the Holy Office. First, he must speak with the governor. However, when he returned to the encampment, he was shocked to learn that Don Luis had been arrested. The captain immediately hastened to Mexico City to the jail.

"Governor, I am truly distressed to see you in this situation. Can I be of some help?" He leaned closer and whispered to Don Luis, "Your fears about the family are well-founded. Trust me — I shall stand by you."

"All is lost — lost!" The governor wearily shook his head. "How could I have been so stupid to bring these heretics to this land? I am a good Christian, devoted to our Savior."

"I know that, Sir. You are, unfortunately, a victim of circumstances. I shall act on your behalf, at once," Nunez assured him.

"Thank you, *Capitain*, you are a true friend, but your efforts will be in vain. I fear the Holy Office is determined to destroy me, at the instigation of my archenemy, Viceroy Zuniga."

Learning of their uncle's imprisonment, Luis and Baltasar visited him in prison and tried to make peace with him, not only because of the familial connection but also because they were afraid that he would report his suspicions about the family. They brought him linens and gifts of food but the irate prisoner rejected them. "I want nothing from you. I rue the day I ever set eyes on any of my sister's family." He turned away from them.

"But, Uncle, we wish to help," Luis said.,

"Help?" Don Luis raged. "You idiots — you are my death warrant. There is only one thing you can do. Stay away from me. I advise you to get down on your knees and pray to Jesus Christ for your salvation."

Luis hastily assured him, "We shall do so at once, Uncle. The entire family shall proclaim their love and devotion to the Savior and we shall pray for your deliverance."

"I want no prayers from you or your 'blind' family." Then as an afterthought, he added, "Give me back all the money I spent for supplies for your mother and father which they never repaid. Now, get out!" he screamed.

On March 7, 1589, Captain Felipe Nunez appeared before the Inquisition for questioning. His relationship with the governor and his family had not gone unnoticed. The Holy Office decided he might be a useful witness in their case against the de Carvajals, and rightly so. Felipe had come to a decision. He confided to Licentiate Santos Garcia, "I have served at Governor de Carvajal's side for several years and enjoy a long friendship with his niece Isabel and her family."

"Captain, would you say they are devoted, practicing Catholics?" asked Garcia.

"To tell the truth, I always found the governor's behavior exemplary, above reproach, a good Christian." Felipe quickly defended his superior.

"And Dona Francisca and her children?" the prelate pursued.

Felipe knew that what he was about to say would deal a mortal blow to the de Carvajal family, but his concern now was mainly for his own safety. He wondered how much they knew of his relationship with Isabel. Evasively, he answered, "I cannot speak for the family but having spent a lot of time with Isabel, the widowed daughter, I recall that on several occasions she asked me questions about my beliefs and asked me to join her in prayer, but I refused."

Garcia sat quietly for a moment and then demanded, "Did she ever speak with you about the God of the Law of Moses?"

Felipe decided to cleanse his conscience. "Yes. On one occasion, Isabel tried to convince me that the Messiah had not yet come and that I must believe in the God of the Law of Moses to find salvation. However, sir, I assure you I firmly resisted any conversion. I believe in the Lord Jesus Christ, the Redeemer, and shall spend my life devoted to Him, as did my parents and their parents before me." He crossed himself.

The licentiate pursed his lips, pressed the palms of his hands together and narrowed his eyes. Silently, he studied the man before him. *Why*, he wondered, *would this man wait so long to report this to the Inquisition. Surely, he knows the law.* "Tell me, Captain, why did you linger so long and say nothing of your exposure to Isabel's proselytizing? You are aware, I believe, that knowledge of such practices makes it incumbent on you to bring this information to the Holy Office."

The captain was quick to reply. "In matters such as these, one must be sure. I went along with everything, of necessity, to fool them, you understand. To be honest, the governor had asked me to ferret out anything of a suspicious nature in the family's activities. As soon as I was convinced of my suspicions, I returned to my post only to find that the governor had been arrested. May I say that he is a good man, a true follower of the Church." He waited for a comment from Garcia. None was forthcoming.

Felipe squirmed. His neck felt moist beneath his collar.

The licentiate remained silent. He was thinking that the captain had proved of value. Obviously, the family were worshippers of the Old Religion. Yet, according to Captain Nunez, not the governor but, for the present, the governor was his primary target. Viceroy Zuniga was emphatic about that. He had approached the inquisitors with information he had gotten from a Franciscan friar in the Huaxteca region who had ridden with the governor on expeditions and met some members of the family. The friar was the one who suggested that perhaps the governor's ancestry should be investigated. Garcia knew that an indictment of the governor would be based more on hearsay and contrived accusations than actual evidence.

Garcia closed in on the captain. "Are you willing to bear witness before the High Tribunal of the Holy Office against any member of the de Carvajal family? Remember your duty as a Catholic."

The captain realized the price that was at stake here. "Of course, of course, my word as an officer."

"This will include testimony against the governor, if necessary, you understand. You testify that he is a good Christian. That may be true but if he harbored *Judaizers*, then he is guilty of a crime." Garcia pressed for firmer commitment. "Remember, if you had any knowledge..." His voice trailed off in an unspoken threat.

To Nunez' credit, even with the inquisitor's insinuating comment, he attempted to avoid an absolute accusation. "As I have said, I have neither seen nor heard anything with respect to the governor that would indicate that. I believe he was suspicious and desired to learn the truth. He would eventually have brought it before the High Tribunal."

Garcia would have appreciated a more accusatory response but, for the moment, it sufficed. *The captain will comply when the time comes, I am sure*, he

mused. *No need to pursue this any further. They had their man.*
Felipe walked out of the Hall of the Inquisition a free man.

Governor de Carvajal stood before the inquisitorial court, a broken man, as he pled his case. "Sirs, I beg you to consider my unfailing loyalty to the Crown and my unwavering devotion to the Catholic Church. My record of achievements speaks for itself —"

The inquisitor cut him off. "We are not concerned with your record."

The governor interjected, "Please hear me out. My service as an admiral and my accomplishments as a conquistador — a leader and sponsor of many expeditions — resulted in much land and wealth for the Royal Court. The King appointed me governor of Nuevo Leon —"

A second inquisitor cut him off. "You are a prisoner of the Holy Office accused of the crime of aiding, abetting, and concealing Jewish apostates."

"Sirs, I implore you! I knew nothing of this Judaizing. My parents and grandparents were good Christians, as am I. I have built churches —"

"Enough!" the inquisitor admonished. He instructed the amanuensis to read the record aloud.

A sweeping denunciation followed, citing testimonies of "certain witnesses". Then the sentence was read: the prisoner shall spend a year in prison in Mexico City and then be exiled from the Spanish colonial territories for six years.

Viceroy Zuniga closed his eyes and muttered to himself, "At last."

CHAPTER VIII

IN PERIL

When Isabel alerted her brothers to Felipe's potential treachery, she urged them to hasten to Mexico City to the family. "I shall stay behind so as not to attract any unnecessary attention," she suggested.

Luis implored her to leave with them. "We fear for your safety, sister. Please come with us now."

"No, no. It would look suspicious if all of us left together suddenly." Isabel tried to reassure Luis, "In a few weeks I shall take Miguel out of school on the pretext that his mother is ill and wishes to see him. Then we shall leave to join you."

"Isabel, you cannot remain here alone. You cannot afford the luxury of waiting, even for a few weeks. Please join us! Pack your most precious belongings. Baltasar and I will go to the school for Miguel," Luis insisted. "Time is of the essence. If you stay and are called by the Holy Office, how shall we be able to help you? Please, I beg you — leave with us."

"Dear brothers, I shall join you shortly, I promise. Perhaps it would be a good idea to take Miguel with you. Yes, that might be best."

Luis argued, "Isabel, do not be blinded in your feelings for that scoundrel Felipe. You are a foolish woman to do so. I am afraid that is why you wish to stay. It is too dangerous!"

Isabel's stubborn streak coupled with a fierce independence and a tendency toward romantic fantasies caused her to underestimate her personal danger. The truth was that she secretly prayed that Felipe would reconsider and return to her. 'Foolish woman' she was, indeed, for at that moment Felipe was professing his devotion to Jesus Christ and denouncing Isabel before the Inquisitiion.

Luis and Baltasar had no problem convincing the Sisters at the Jesuit school that their mother was ill and asking for Miguel. They promised to return him to the school within two weeks.

The brothers stopped by to see Isabel before leaving for Mexico City and it was a sad parting, full of apprehensions. As they kissed each other, their tears intermingled. "Soon, sister, come soon. Do not delay," Luis urged.

On the road, they moved slowly and unobtrusively, ever watchful. They found room and board with other Secret Jews and spent time in prayer with them. Luis conducted the meetings and also taught them some of his original compositions. The slow pace of their journey allowed them to visit with families in several small towns. They took advantage of the opportunity to engage in as much business as possible, selling linens, clothing, household items and silverware. They were also able to collect some of the debts owed them by merchants. It was essential that they raise as much money as possible in case a quick escape became necessary. Luis knew that the fleet was leaving from Vera Cruz in the near future and planned to book passage for the family.

On the evening before they planned to reach Mexico City while they were staying with friends, a messenger came with news of the arrests of Gaspar and Isabel. They had arrested Gaspar — a priest? And poor Isabel! Why had she not listened to him? Luis was distraught. He suggested to his brothers, "Perhaps we should make arrangements to leave at once. It might be easier to exert influence with some of our family's friends in Europe who could intercede for us. It seems that the Holy Office is determined to arrest all the de Carvajals. With the proper influence from abroad, we may be able to save ourselves." He waited for Baltasar to speak.

"I agree. We must leave at once. Let us make haste to Vera Cruz where we will be able to book passage on a ship joining the fleet from Tierra Firma."

"Good. There is no time to lose. Vamanos," answered Luis.

As they proceeded to Vera Cruz, Luis struggled with his conscience. Finally, he decided on a course of action and told his brother, "Baltasar, you and Miguel must go but I cannot leave our mother and siblings. I shall remain and do my best to protect them. If we are arrested, you will receive news of it, I am sure. Then you must use all available favors from friends."

"Please, Luis — come with us. You will be of more help from abroad. If they imprison you, what will you be able to accomplish?"

"I shall give strength to our mother and sisters by my presence. Go with God, my loved ones." He bent down to kiss his little brother's brow. "Be brave, little Miguel."

Miguel soberly accepted the show of love and advice. He did not question the sagacity of his brother's decision. All he knew was that he did not understand why this was happening and he began to cry.

"When shall we meet again, my dear Luis?" The elder brother was in tears, as well.

Luis answered softly, "If not in this world, then on the glory road to God, to salvation. Go in peace, both of you. We shall all be together again someday." They embraced.

Turning his horse in the direction of Mexico City, Luis looked back at his loved ones standing so forlornly in the road and waved a farewell. Then he urged his horse to a gallop and was soon out of sight.

Luis did not relish the trip that lay ahead. The rainy season was beginning and that would add to the difficulty of traveling; however, he was familiar with the terrain, having made many trips with his father and brother on business to some of the towns in the vicinity. Memories of those trips saddened but comforted Luis. He missed his father and all the good times they had shared. Sorrow overwhelmed him as he recalled the suffering Francisco had endured in those last days. Now the family faced more tragedy. "God, Adonai, help your poor servants in their need," he prayed.

His horse was fine as they rode across the lowlands but Luis knew that when they came to the mountain paths, he would have to proceed with the utmost caution. The way was rugged and could be slippery. "But," he observed, "the view is stupendous." He had almost forgotten how beautiful the landscape was, how the abundant, colorful flowers and stately trees were interrupted occasionally by clear, little refreshing streams. The magnificence of it all almost made him forget momentarily as he stopped now and then to admire the vista and drink some of the cool, fresh water.

He thought, *I understand the natives' love for this land and how they nurtured it. To them, Mother Earth was a god to be revered and their gods and the land were one. Not so their conquerors!* Luis shook his head. *They took from the land everything it had to offer and did not return an iota of respect for all it yielded.* He took a deep breath and rode on.

It was the year 1589 and Luis, at 22 years of age, was in the unenviable position of fugitive, having committed the "crime" of clinging to the faith he fervently believed to be the true one. He and his family were facing the possibility of an inquisitorial audience. He wondered what had already happened to his sister and brother. As for Uncle Luis, the governor, he could only hope that he had not betrayed the family and, too, that he himself was not in danger. *It is sad to say,* thought Luis, *but I thank God that my father did not live to see this turn of events.*

Finally, a weary Luis and his worn out horse reached the bowl-shaped valley in which Mexico City nestled. As he sat mounted on his horse, he looked every inch the conquistador — strong, proud, and determined. Only his mind and heart felt the strain of worry and his body, the fatigue of the journey. *I shall see my mother soon,* he meditated, *and that makes me happy.* That brief moment was destroyed by the realization of what might be in store. A cry escaped his lips. "Oh, God, my mother! My sweet, gentle Mother!" He could not bear the thought of her suffering before the High Tribunal. *Dear God,* he prayed, *let me have enough time."*

Dona Francisca had moved to a little apartment of her own near the Canal Gate, which was close to the Great Square and the cathedral. Mariana lived with her and attended the School for Girls nearby. Francisca had taken the apartment when her sons-in-law had moved to Taxco for business reasons. The move was not to be a permanent one, so Francisca opted to stay in Mexico City with Mariana. Leonor, Catalina,and Anica stayed as well, because Jorge and Antonio thought it wise not to uproot them.

When she heard of the arrests of Isabel and Gaspar, Francisca tried not to panic. What could she do? *If only my boys were here...*

I can only sit and wait and pray.

As Luis carefully approached the perimeter of the Great Square, he was anguished by the thought that his reunion with his family was fraught with danger. He kept to the side streets because tonight the Square was buzzing with activity. It was a feast day honoring the Virgin Mary and the city was celebrating. The *"mascarado"* (grand parade) was just ending; people were dancing and singing as clowns, acrobats and jugglers followed the colorful floats around the Square. Musicians played lively music while happy strollers joked and laughed. From a dark corner, Luis observed how church dignitaries and royal officers mingled with the crowd, a constant reminder of the ever-presence of Mother Church. Priests swung their censers which filled the air with incense that wafted over the revelers. Criollos, mestivos, mulattoes, peninsulares, all dressed in their finery, enjoying the occasion and happy in the thought that salvation was theirs.

When Luis knocked at his mother's door, Francisca jumped from her chair, calling out, *"Quien es?* Who is there, *por favor?"* She hastened to the window and peeked into the darkness. Her heart leaped with joy when she heard, "Mother, it is I, Luis."

Flinging the door open, she nervously pulled him inside, and bolted the door behind them. "My beloved son, my darling boy, my brave one. I am both overjoyed and deeply troubled to see you."

"Madre, I knew of the arrests."

"Oh, God!" she exclaimed. "Tell me, where is Baltasar? Miguel?"

Luis explained what had transpired in Tampico, how they left Isabel at her insistence. Francisca wept when he told her of the parting of the brothers on the way to Vera Cruz.

"Why did you not go with them? At least you would be free from these devils." Francisca was uncontrollable and when he tried to console her, she asked, "What shall we do?"

"Be strong, dear Mother. Come, let us pray together." But Francisca could not cease her crying. Luis took her in his arms, holding her tenderly, speaking softly, trying to bring her solace. They sat together late into the night. When she fell asleep, he carried her to her bed, gently placed a blanket over her and kissed her tear-stained cheeks. He looked down at her lovingly and whispered, "God grant you sweet dreams this night."

Luis did not sleep. His mind raced from one possibility to another, seeking, hoping, praying for a solution. He could not comprehend this nightmare. He asked God, "How many more millennia must pass before Your promise to Israel is fulfilled and we are delivered from our oppressors?

Finally, at last, sleep came.

In the morning, Francisca found her son still slumbering on the couch. She tiptoed to the kitchen and, as quietly as possible, prepared something to eat. Before she tapped him on the shoulder and softly called his name, she stood for a minute wondering, *What will become of this wonderful boy of mine? He is so good, so bright and holds such promise. What will happen to all of us?*

"Luis, my son, let us have something to eat. We must prepare ourselves to deal with our predicament."

"Good morning, Madre. I shall wash quickly and join you at the table." He kissed her.

As they ate their breakfast, they discussed the possibilities of what might occur should they be arrested. Luis proposed a plan of defense to shield the family. If only he knew what or how much information the Holy Office had or who had given testimony against them. They did not have time to ponder the question. A loud knock at the door dispelled all thoughts but instant fear. Francisca clutched at Luis' arm as he rose to see who it was.

When he carefully opened the door, two bailiffs, a constable, and a notary pushed their way into the house. "Luis de Carvajal, el Mozo, and Dona Francisca de Carvajal, you are under arrest by order of the Holy Office of the Inquisition." The loud voice of the constable brought Leonor, Catalina and Anica onto the scene just as their mother and brother were being led away. Their screams rent the air.

Dona Francisca was a woman of courage and dignity and she responded in like manner to her captors. Her daughters' screams caused her grief and she tried to calm them by remaining stoic. "It is nothing, my darlings," she called to them. "Just some questions to answer. We shall return in a little while." As she turned to go, she uttered a prayer to the Almighty for the opportunity to prove her faith.

Luis cried out, "God shall reveal the truth. Do not fear, my sisters. Be strong."

They were taken to Casa Chata (Flat House) where the maximum security compound — the secret cells — played psychological havoc with prisoners' minds. The warden, Arias de Valdes, ushered Luis into a dank, dark underground compartment. Only a candle provided a flickering light by which he could barely discern the dimensions of the room. He wondered where Isabel and his mother were. In a hole in hell such as this? What terrors awaited them in this house of horrors? He shuddered as he recalled stories of the inhuman treatment and suffering of prisoners at the hand of the Inquisition. He immediately altered his course of thinking. The situation called for courage and a clear head.

The next interminable hours were spent mostly in prayer. Dozing off now and then, he was plagued by disturbing dreams. Only the jailer came to his door to bring some food, most of which Luis did not eat.

Two days later, he was summoned to his first interrogation. As he stood before his inquisitors, Dr. Hernandez Bonilla and Licentiate Santos Garcia (a prosecuting attorney for the Holy Office), Luis masked the dread he felt. The inquisitors were seated behind a long table upon which were a variety of documents and several tall, lit candelabra. Nearby sat an amanuensis who recorded every question and answer. Flanking the inquisitors were two members of the clergy. The candles flickered and cast eerie shadows across the large, stone hall and the stern faces, whose piercing eyes and thin-lined lips threatened unspoken imminent danger.

The panel of men was surprised at the outward calmness and self-assurance of their prisoner. Luis had an air of dignity and self-worth about him that amazed them. No groveling, sniveling penitent here. This de Carvajal would surely prove to be a formidable adversary. Suddenly, Bonilla stated, "I will address several issues regarding your behavior and beliefs. Let me warn you, Luis de Carvajal, *el Mozo*, that you must deal with us in a truthful manner."

Luis knew full well that he had to be most watchful of any entrapment. He answered, "I shall tell the Court the truth as it is."

The next words from Bonilla, uttered harshly and bluntly, almost caught Luis off his guard. "When did you start to worship the God of the Law of Moses?"

"I am a believer in the Lord Jesus Christ, my Savior." The answer came swiftly and simply, totally surprising them.

"Do you deny taking part in secret family rituals — rituals of the Jews?"

"Sir, I have been educated in Jesuit schools and believe in the teachings of our Lord Jesus Christ. Our family has practiced Catholicism for generations."

"You are aware, are you not, that your brother Gaspar is in custody, as well as your sister Isabel?" Bonilla waited for a reaction.

"Yes," answered Luis, "and I tell you they are as devout in their Christian beliefs as am I. My brother Gaspar is a man of the cloth and has dedicated his life to the Evangelical Law of the Church."

Garcia spoke next and said something that shocked Luis. "If you are so dedicated then why did your sister Isabel admit that she is a follower of the Old Religion?"

Luis showed no reaction but it was quite a blow to learn of her admission. He weighed his next words carefully. "My sister is dedicated to Christ, the Lord. I have never seen nor heard differently." At least now he had some idea of what he had to contend with.

Bonilla countered with, "Her confession indicated that she even tried to convince your uncle to return to the Dead Law, the Old Religion. In fact, the governor confirmed her story. How do you explain that?"

Ever evasive, Luis answered, "I can only say that my uncle said these things because he hates us. This is the truth of the matter." Luis resorted to this excuse because he had heard it said that if the Court believed that hatred was the motive for a witness' statement, it would sometimes release prisoners on that premise.

The inquisitors, now angered and frustrated, ordered the jailer to return the prisoner to his cell. They said nothing to him at first but, as they turned to go, Luis heard the words that were to cause him unbearable anguish.

"Perhaps your mother will provide additional enlightenment. Obviously you are not willing to cooperate." Garcia stared at him for a moment and then he and the others exited by a side door. Luis was dragged away to his solitary confinement.

Back in his cell, huddled in a corner, he spent hours in prayer, asking for help. He did not know that the court actuary, invoking the name of Jesus Christ, had read the sentence that Francisca Nunez de Carvajal was to be put to torment and that, in fact, she was already in the torture chamber not too far from his cell. Later, as he dozed fitfully, the sounds of sobbing and pleading shattered the stillness of the night and he recognized his mother's voice. The feeling of helplessness that enveloped him, enraged him. The fiends! How could they do this to a defenseless woman? No doubt these evil monsters intentionally put him in this dark hole close to the torture chamber, to intimidate him and intensify his suffering. All he could do was ask God, Adonai, to help her endure her trials and hope that his mother's faith would sustain her.

When the screaming and entreaties stopped, Luis wondered if his mother had survived. It was so quiet now. Suddenly, he heard two jailers talking outside his door. Luis pressed his ear against it.

"Let us get her back to her cell," one said. "She is strong, all right. Thought she would have fainted hours ago. I have seen some who did not live through the torture. A strong one, for sure." The jailers moved on.

"Thank you, thank you, Dios mio, my mother is alive." Luis whispered in the darkness. He felt such relief, such gratitude for her deliverance, such agony for her pain.

A plan. A plan. He must devise one to save them.

CHAPTER IX

VIGILS AND VISIONS

Juan Rodriquez de Silva was a close friend of the de Carvajals and he resided in Mexico City. The news of the arrests caused him much distress. He slept fitfully at night and moved about cautiously by day. This was the way of life for Secret Jews. Knowing the modis operandi of the Inquisition from reports of those who had appeared before the Holy Tribunal, he was aware of the horrendous conditions of the 'secret cells' and of the acts of horror within those walls. *Whose mind was strong enough, whose body was strong enough to withstand the cruelty meted out,* he often wondered. He had heard that under intolerable conditions, many a helpless victim had even implicated his own family. How terrible! He shrank from the thought. Now he wondered, *How long before they come for me — how long?*

A loud, insistent knocking at the door late one night caused him, literally, to jump from his bed. He quietly stole to the window and tried to discern who the two figures were standing on his doorstep. Only when he heard the familiar secret greeting, "We are from good people" did he sigh with relief and hasten to open the door.

"Baltasar, Miguel! My dear friends, what brings you here at this hour?" He embraced them in a big bear hug. "Sit down, amigos. Tell me all."

"Juan, my friend, we had plans Luis and I to get the family out of here to safety. You have heard, no doubt, of what has happened?"

Juan nodded. *"Seguramente."*

Baltasar continued. "Upon hearing about Isabel and our uncle, Luis insisted on coming back alone to Mexico City to be with our dear mother and sisters. The three of us were already on our way to Vera Cruz to escape by ship, but Luis would not leave. Miguel and I were supposed to continue to the port and secure passage to Europe but we had a talk and decided to remain and go into hiding and await developments."

"Why did you not save yourselves?" Juan asked. "What can you accomplish by staying?"

Baltasar explained, "We need to find out first what the charges are against the family if we are to get any help abroad. Even our brother Gaspar has been arrested."

"Yes, I know," Juan answered, "but you know they will deal with him separately to avoid the embarrassment of bringing a Dominican friar to public trial."

'Now, sadly, we must also await news of Luis and our mother." Baltasar hung his head despondently. Then he asked, "If you do not object, Juan, my little brother and I shall stay here with you until we learn some news and are able to decide what steps we must take."

Juan sat across from them, his hands folded in his lap, looking forlorn. Baltasar knew he was asking a lot. His friend was torn between two devils. How could he refuse to give them shelter? And yet if he were investigated and discovered to be harboring de Carvajals, he would be charged with Judaizing and maybe more.

"Juan, this is too much to ask of you. I do not wish to put you in jeopardy. We shall leave."

"No, no, amigo," Juan quickly responded. "You are as brothers to me. Of course, you shall stay as long as you have need to. We shall exercise great caution, that is all. Mi casa es su casa. It does not look good for us. The Inquisition has intensified its activities since Viceroy Zuniga's return. The Holy Office is now relentless in tracking down Secret Jews. Ah, Baltasar, it seems that this evil follows us even across vast seas. We must pray to Adonai and take hope that this too shall pass."

"Amen," echoed the brothers, in unison, shamelessly wiping away tears.

Juan poured a glass of wine for each of them, even for little Miguel, and exclaimed warmly, "Welcome, my brothers! To life!"

Several days later, one of Juan's cousins confirmed the sad news that Luis and his mother had been taken to Casa Chata. *How long before they arrest my sisters?* Baltasar wondered. "I wish I could go to them but right now, there is nothing to do but wait."

It was a long, difficult vigil and they had to content themselves with morsels of news that filtered in occasionally. The months seemed endless. They could only imagine what suffering their loved ones were enduring. As more and more time passed, they anticipated the worst and then they heard that their sisters had been arrrested and subjected to intense interrogation, even little eight-year old Anica. From what the cousin could gather, the girls had been firm in their denials of any forbidden practices — until they were read the confessions of their mother and Isabel. At that point, he heard, they had broken down. Little Anica was placed in protective custody with a

Catholic family for "proper care and instruction" and her sisters were sent to the secret cells.

Baltasar and Miguel remained in hiding for one long year, a year spent mostly in the seclusion of the house. This permitted Baltasar to take advantage of the usufruct of Juan's library which contained biblical and prayer books. As they had done so often in the past, they held secret meetings with other Judaizers, including Manuel de Lucena and his wife, close friends of Luis', who were of great religious fervor and devoted to proselytizing. Luis would want it so, they agreed.

It was customary for a relative or friend to bring articles of clothing and food to prisoners and to pay for their room and board in spite of the fact that their money and property had been confiscated when they were imprisoned. In Luis' case, the Inquisition had seized almost all that the de Carvajals possessed, even to the coins in Luis' pockets that first night in Casa Chata. Juan's cousin would often visit the jail on the pretext of leaving something for the family. In this way, he hoped to glean tidbits of information.

One of the jailers, a rotund and rather comical-looking fellow, became quite talkative when he discovered that a friendly "chat" would benefit him monetarily.

"Indeed, *Senor*," he confided one day, "the family has been subjected to the torture chamber, I hear. The confessions forced out of them have doomed them, I am afraid. Only Luis is still under interrogation. In fact, he has had his second audience. I hear the judges are frustrated because he remains unshaken. The fellow is a tower of strength."

The cousin, trying to perpetuate the myth, replied, "I do not understand. The family — all of them — they are good Christians. What are the charges, do you know?"

"I hear that all but Luis have admitted to Judaizing. They tried to hold out but trips to the torture chamber were too much for the poor things. All I can say is they are being charged with heresy. That is what I hear, Senor." He paused, then added, "I must move on now. I promise you we shall talk again." He walked brusquely away, surreptitiously pocketing the ducats carefully slipped into his hand a few moments before.

Days and nights blended and lost their meaning. Luis remained in his dark cubicle, hardly eating, rarely sleeping, barely existing. Most of the time he was deep in thought, trying to formulate some plan for survival. He longed for a book of prayers to sustain him spiritually but had to content himself with repeating, over and over again, the prayers he knew from memory and those which he had written himself. Luis longed to read the psalms of the prophet David but he knew that acquiring any such books was an impossibility for him.

On most Saturdays, inquisitors visited with the prisoners, either to get confessions or bring about conversions — or both. In anticipation of these visits, the cells would be cleaned. This was the only time that the occupants were permitted a breath of fresh air and to walk about the courtyard of the jail. One particular Saturday, a judge of the Holy Tribunal came to visit Luis. He had with him a Franciscan friar. "Luis, this is Padre Ruiz de Luna who will be sharing your cell."

Luis was surprised but said nothing. He wondered what crime the friar had committed. There was a brief exchange of greetings and just before the judge left, the friar requested, "Please, may I request that a breviary be brought to me?" The judge acquiesced and left. Later, when a jailer delivered the book, Luis thought that surely it was an act of Divine Intervention. The good friar suggested, "Luis, you may borrow the book any time you choose. Perhaps it will bring you consolation, my son."

A grateful Luis agreed.

At first, the two men did not share more than polite conversation but after Luis borrowed the breviary several times, the friar commented, "You are truly a man of religious convictions. You read and pray as though you are a man of the cloth."

"Would that I were," Luis commented. "But you are. May I ask why you have been arrested?"

"Well, my son, I am accused of using forged letters of authorization to celebrate mass and I administered other sacraments. Somehow this was discovered and so..." He threw his hands up in a gesture of resignation.

Luis expressed his surprise. "And, yet, the jailer called you 'padre' and you still wear the customary garments of a friar."

"Of course. First they must put me on trial and find me guilty, then they will strip me of everything, eh?"

"Let us pray they will not be successful." Luis tried to be encouraging.

De Luna laughed cynically and then, bluntly, he asked, "Are you of the Christian faith?"

The question astonished Luis. How should he respond? All along he had maintained that he was a true Christian. Recently, he had made some decisions and he had other plans now. He told the padre, "I have many questions to which I cannot find answers in the Catholic faith."

This piqued the friar's curiosity. "What sort of questions? What sort of answers do you seek?"

Luis studied the man for several minutes. This situation may work in his favor considering the course of action upon which he had decided. He might as well test the waters. "I come from a family of "conversos," a fact I never knew until I was thirteen years old. I had always believed that we were Catholic, until my father, God rest his soul, revealed to me that although we lived as Christians, in reality we were Secret Jews. I learned this on our voyage from the Iberian Peninsula on my uncle's ship. My uncle was Governor Luis de Carvajal y de la Cueva."

The friar interjected. "You say 'was'. Is he deceased?"

"Yes. My uncle was arrested and imprisoned shortly before I was. He was accused of harboring Secret Jews; they indicted him and sentenced him to a year in prison and then exile for six years. I heard that he somehow mysteriously died in prison six months after his confinement — a big, strapping figure of a man like him — it is strange."

"But you Luis, you say you had no knowledge of the family's Jewish practices until your trip to the New World?"

"That is true. I attended Jesuit schools and one of my older brothers, Gaspar, was sent to the priesthood. I had no reason to ever consider the possibility of being a Jew."

The friar was puzzled. "So why are you here now?"

"Once I learned the truth, I was overwhelmed with a voracious desire to learn as much as possible about the Law which God handed down to Moses. This I was able to do through instruction and information I received from my mentor, Dr. Morales, to whom my father entrusted my indoctrination during our voyage. Once here in New Spain, I secretly continued my studies and held meetings with other 'conversos' who wished to exchange ideas and information and to practice the Old Religion — the Mosaic Law.

"My being imprisoned, I believe, is the evil doing of my deceased uncle who was vehemently against the family's secret practices and he probably brought it to the attention of the Inquisition while he was being investigated."

"In your studies of the Mosaic Law," the friar pursued his questioning, "did you find any of the answers you were seeking?"

"Yes, I found what I believe to be the truth," Luis eagerly continued. "In Jesuit school, I was taught to worship the Trinity. This I never questioned until I was tutored by Dr. Morales and he explained the doctrine of the God of the Law of Moses. A whole new religious concept developed in my mind and I yearned for more knowledge."

"What is this doctrine that so affected you?"

Luis explained. "In Deuteronomy, God proclaims that He is One, only One, and He created one man, Adam, so that non-believers could not say that there is more than one power in heaven, for if He had created more than one man, some might argue that there were other deities, that one God alone did not form all of them. To quote, 'I am one and alone in the Universe'."

"How does this destroy the concept of the Trinity?" asked de Luna.

Luis quoted from Isaiah and Exodus: "'I am the first for I have no father, and I am the last for I have no brother, and besides me there is no God for I have no son.'" He looked at the friar, expecting rebuttal.

Instead, the friar urged, "Go on, please — this is most interesting."

Obliging willingly, Luis continued. "God is incorporeal. Like our souls, He is not something tactile but rather ethereal. The place of the Holy One is unknown." He continued to quote. "His knowledge is limitless. He knows all that will be and that is and has been. He is omniscient. God's Holy Law and His words are incorruptible. Even in the Gospel, it is told that your Crucified One said that it would be easier for the sky or earth to be missing than a jot or tittle of this Holy Law."

Friar de Luna was amazed at Luis' ability to quote verbatim from the books of the Bible. "I should like to ponder our discussion," he told Luis. "May we continue tomorrow?"

"Of course, padre."

Luis felt energized for the first time since his imprisonment. At last — someone with whom he could discuss that which was closest to his heart! Adonai, blessed be His name, had provided him with an undertaking — perhaps the conversion of the friar?

As the days passed, Luis and de Luna sat long hours discussing theology. When the friar displayed some doubts about his own religious convictions, Luis pursued the Mosaic Law with vigorous argumentation. He narrated stories of the great achievements of Biblical heroes. The cleric, who had little knowledge of the Old Religion or its figures of strength and courage, was deeply impressed.

In time, de Luna noticed that Luis was growing frail and weak. He attributed this to the fact that he spent many days fasting and praying and even when he did eat, he ate only vegetables, fruit and tortillas or other breads but he rejected lard or anything prepared with it.

"Luis," he asked, "why do you abstain from certain foods? You are not eating enough to keep a fly aloft."

Happy to explain, Luis referred to Leviticus 11 wherein the Lord ordained which beasts and fowl were unclean (not to be eaten) and which were clean; also, which creatures in the sea were allowed or forbidden as food.

De Luna was fascinated and said, with sincerity, "Luis, hereafter I, too, shall reject these forbidden foods. After all you have revealed to me, I believe that the Lord has enlightened me and I am now ready to accept 'the divine truth'."

Together, they prayed and praised God and gave thanks: Luis, for having converted the padre and the padre, for having found his way to this holy knowledge.

It was shortly thereafter that Luis started having visionary dreams — dreams which brought him much comfort and gave him strength. The first vision concerned his beloved mother. An aged wise man appeared and told him, "While your mother was sweet and innocent before the Lord, she exuded a fragrance like a flower and now, ill-treated and abused by her judges, she exudes great strength before the Lord."

Luis awoke, comforted, and gave thanks to the Almighty for bringing him consolation. The next night, Luis had another vision. King Solomon stood before him with a vial of liquid and instructed him to drink from it. "This is the nectar of wisdom and the Lord wishes you to drink it down." Luis did as he was told and felt strangely at peace. When he awoke, he told his companion of his dreams. The friar asked him if he knew what these dreams meant.

"I believe I do," Luis said. "God wishes me to devote my life to His truth and to lead others to the Mosaic Law. From now on I shall be known as Joseph Lumbroso..."

De Luna interrupted. "I do not understand, I am afraid. What does —?"

Luis explained, "Joseph after the biblical Joseph, the dreamer and visionary, the patriarch of his people and Lumbroso, which means the light-bearer, the enlightened."

"*Bueno*, my boy," the friar responded enthusiastically.

Luis smiled for the first time in months.

Early one morning, several months later, the warden suddenly opened the door to Luis' cell and instructed the friar to gather his things together. "You are ordered to appear before the Court immediately," he was told.

The friar complied. Turning to Luis, he told him, "I shall leave my breviary with you to bring you comfort. God be with you." They exchanged meaningful glances.

"God be with you," echoed Luis.

As the friar stood before the inquisitors, the first question hurled at him was one he had expected.

"Well, Friar de Luna, what information do you have for us about your cellmate? Is he a heretic?"

The friar answered softly, "Sir, I have spent long hours with the youth but he gave me no indication of an abandonment of the faith. We read together from the breviary and prayed together. Luis de Carvajal was most fervent in this and I can tell you I heard nothing that would indict him."

Puzzled, Inquisitor Bonilla regarded him for a moment and then announced, "It is too bad that you have proven useless to us. We had hoped there would be no reason to proceed with the charges against you." He signaled the amanuensis to swear in the friar.

CHAPTER X

THE SENTENCE

Luis knew his third appearance before the High Tribunal would be a crucial one. If it did not produce the desired results, the prosecuting attorney would have the prerogative to request that the prisoner be subjected to torture.

When he faced the inquisitors, he was asked the same question as before: "Luis de Carvajal, are you an observer of the Dead Law of Moses?"

"No, Sirs, I am not. I am a devout Christian and practice the tenet of the Christian faith."

"What is the tenet of the Christian faith?"

"It is the belief in the Holy Trinity."

"What is meant by the Holy Trinity?"

"It is the true nature of God," answered Luis.

Alonso de Peralta, the inquisitor assigned to conduct this third interrogation, asked, "And what is this true nature?"

"It is that of a God of three persons," defined Luis, "the Father, the Son and the Holy Ghost." Luis maintained a calm demeanor outwardly, but inwardly he sensed this man was someone to be feared, more so than the others. He continued, "Christianity is the true faith in which I shall find salvation."

Peralta was amazed that this prisoner remained so staunch. As the questioning continued, the judges and prelates were impressed. Their circumlocution reaped no harvest. Luis eluded every trap of confession. He would confess to no apostasy. The inquisitor, visibly irritated by the unsuccessful interview, agreed with the prosecutor's recommendation that Luis follow the path of others who were recalcitrant. He relegated Luis to the torture chamber.

The cruelties to which they subjected him were beyond human endurance. Only Luis' prayers gave him the strength to surmount the excruciating pain of the ropes tightening around his body and the rack which stretched his limbs and almost tore him apart. In his delirium, he imagined himself removed from this dungeon. A vision came to him in which he saw himself standing before a virtuous and wise man who placed his hand upon Luis' head, blessed him and advised, "Remember thy covenant with the Lord and He will not forsake thee."

As the priests in the torture chamber stood by urging him to confess to spare himself further pain, Luis clung to his vision in a trance, and spoke not a word.

Luis had made a decision the day the jailer had come for Friar de Luna. It was time to take the gamble that might save them, but first he must get some information about the friar's fate. Had de Luna exposed their discussions and his own conversion to Judaism? Luis was deeply concerned, for such divulgence would impact his plan. Luckily, Diego de Espinosa, the "friendly" guard, was on duty near Luis' cell the next night. The loquacious fellow himself known to Luis by leaning against the cell door and, sotto voce, telling him about his cousin's visits. When Luis asked him about the friar, Diego's tongue was loosened by the prospect of gold ducats. He confided that de Luna had been sentenced on the original charge against him, of holding fraudulent papers to the Franciscan Order that he had obtained in Italy — nothing else.

Luis felt a surge of relief. The padre had not betrayed him. He told the jailer, "You shall receive a proper recompense for your trouble, my friend. Tell my visitor when he returns that you spoke with me and I said, 'God will provide'. He will see to it that you are rewarded."

In the early hours before dawn, several nights later, guards on duty in the secret cells were alarmed by cries and shouts from Luis' cell. Upon entering, they found him on his knees, begging for an audience before the Holy Tribunal. The wardens quieted him and promised to take him to his inquisitors as soon as possible. Luis, still kneeling, beat his chest and intoned the old familiar chant, "Mea culpa, mea culpa," the admission of guilt.

The guards, dumb struck by the radical change in the prisoner's behavior, rushed to relate the news to the Holy Office. The late hour did not matter in such instances. The judges lost no time in summoning a recorder, two witnesses, the prosecuting attorney and the attorney assigned to Luis. All hastened to Casa Chata. Apparently, a recantation was about to take place. They would lose no time in getting there for fear that the prisoner might have a change of heart.

Peralta and the others were shocked at Luis' appearance and behavior. Gone was the self-assurance and stubborn denial of previous meetings. He stood before them, head drooping, tears in his eyes as he stated, "I know I deserve your condemnation for my deceptions and lies but I beg for your mercy for I have been in the clutches of the devil. Now I have seen the light and am free to speak." Luis' hands were clenched in supplication as he entreated the judges.

Relishing the moment, Peralta snarled at him, "What do you wish to confess?"

Luis fell to his knees. "I am guilty of harboring heterodox beliefs contrary to the Catholic Church and I wish to confess that I and my family were possessed by demons and made 'blind' to the true faith. Have mercy on me and my loved ones who were led astray."

"Begin your testimony. I caution you to reveal all that is true," Peralta instructed.

Luis breathed deeply and began. "Before my father died, he revealed to me that I was a Jew and also that my beloved mother, my brother Baltasar, and my sister Isabel were Secret Jews. I ask your kind understanding that my younger siblings had no involvement in these practices." Luis hoped to protect the children. He was not aware that it was too late. Mariana, Leonor, Catalina, and Anica were already in the clutches of the Inquisition.

Peralta interjected, "What of your brother Gaspar, the monk?"

Ever the protector, Luis answered, "While he and I had many discussions on theology — he did question the manner in which my father's corpse was prepared for burial — I believe Gaspar did not surmise that the Old Religion played any part in it. The truth is, what I did conformed with Jewish custom. My father had requested that I do this for him. As for Gaspar, he had no reason to believe we were not good Christians inasmuch as we went to church and confession and took communion regularly."

"And your uncle, the governor," continued the inquisitor, "was he not aware of the family's clandestine activities?"

Luis saw no reason to involve his uncle any longer. Only God could judge him now. "When my sister Isabel tried to convert the governor, he struck her a blow, admonishing her never to speak of the Old Religion again. He shouted at her and swore his devotion to the Lord Jesus Christ. I know he died in that belief." Briefly, his eyes locked with Peralta's.

For the next five days, Luis was subjected to intense interrogation concerning religious doctrine. As he spoke, the panel continued to be amazed at Luis' ability to quote eloquently from the Bible, referencing accurately each passage. He explained, in detail, the rituals and observances practiced by the family during Pascua (Passover) — the eating of the pan cincino (the matzot)

— and the holiday of Shavuot (the Festival of the First Fruits). He explained the importance of Yom Kippur (the Great Day) during which they fasted and atoned for their sins and begged the Almighty to forgive them their trespasses.

When he spoke of his covenant with God, the act of circumcision, Peralta asked, "Why did you perform this act upon yourself?"

Luis replied, "In Genesis 17, it is written that the soul of a man who is not circumcised will be erased from the list of the living. God told this to Abraham and then to Moses. I wanted to be on God's list to assure my entry into Paradise. I confess now that I have been 'blind' and that my salvation and that of my family lies in accepting the Evangelical Law of Jesus Christ." *Right now,* thought Luis, *the 'salvation', the survival of the de Carvajals, was his primary concern. Adonai would deal with their souls when the time came.*

Peralta announced, "The examination of Luis de Carvajal, el Mozo, is now concluded and the case closed. Sentencing will take place tomorrow morning, the 13th day of February, in the year of our Lord, 1590."

The next day, the prisoners were marched, barefoot, from the prison. They wore sleeveless sanbenitos made of yellow sackcloth — knee-length tunics adorned with religious symbols. On the tops of their heads, they wore fools' caps. All carried tall, lighted green candles or green crosses as they were routed in solemn procession through the streets to the cathedral.

Preceding the prisoners was a parade of ecclesiastical dignitaries, royal officials, and the Mayordomo, who carried a large, white cross which represented hope that the souls of those to be "penanced" would find salvation. The crowds cheered the lines of priests and secular officials, shouting praises for their holy work. Advance notice had been posted so the public would attend and now the dignitaries were pleased to see the multitudes milling about. What a glorious affirmation of the faith! As many of the spectators as possible pushed their way into the cathedral to position themselves for the spectacle. The frenzied throng jeered and threw fruits and vegetables at the prisoners as they passed by to take their places.

Reunited with his mother and sisters again, under such horrific circumstances, Luis felt emotionally drained. He longed to throw his arms around them, to hold them in a close embrace, to give them encouragement. As he stood there, so tall and spiritually strong, he resembled a biblical shepherd gathering his flock around him. Francisca could not resist the thought that surely this must be what a messiah would look like.

The guards hastened them to their places on the benches where the penitents sat. Luis' eyes imparted to his loved ones a message of hope: be brave, believe, and the Lord will be your strength. Francisca gazed at her remarkable son and saw the religious fervor still burning intensely, his eyes shining with a passion for life. She whispered her thanks to the Merciful Almighty.

The "auto-da-fe" (act of faith) instilled fear in the strongest of hearts. As an inquisitor read aloud the names and corresponding "sins" and the penalties therefor, Luis wondered how, in God's name, such cruelty could be condoned by holy men.

The *sanbenitos* which the de Carvajals wore were adorned with two red bands forming St. Andrew's cross, the symbol of reconciliation with the Church. In order to reconcile, a prisoner abjured *"de levi"* or *"de vehementi."* Abjuring "de levi" was an oral oath of eternal obedience to the Pope and "de vehementi", a written oath with the acknowledgment that relapsing to the Old Religion would carry the penalty of death if "relapsos" were tried and found guilty.

The High Tribunal announced that it had proven its case against the de Carvajals and found them guilty of heresy, as charged. In addition, they decreed that Francisco de Matos (Luis' father) and his brother Baltasar and Miguel to be impenitents and ordered them burned in effigy — the father, posthumously; the brothers, in absentia. Luis and the other members of the family were deemed to be penitents — all had begged for mercy and indicated a willingness to abjure and be reconciled to the "true faith." All had abjured "de vehementi." Peralta had made certain of that.

As the family stood before the Court, Luis looked at his loved ones and their eyes showed the relief they felt. Almighty God had spared them.

Luis was sentenced to 'perpetual' prison and the wearing of the penitential cloak (the sanbenito) for the duration of his sentence, the length of which would be on-going until otherwise decided. His mother and Isabel received surprisingly heavy sentences. They would be obliged to wear sanbenitos for the rest of their lives. Mariana, only fifteen years of age, received one year in 'prison and garb' while her older sisters, Leonor and Catalina, received two. Where the sentences were to be served would be determined by the judges. Little Anica, because she was only nine was not present at the proceedings. She had been placed in protective custody with the family of Pedro de los Rios, the Inquisitional secretary, to assure her upbringing in the Catholic faith.

Gaspar, along with a few clerics who were convicted of attempting seduction in the confessional, received a reprimand in a private hearing. His crime was determined to be that of not reporting his suspicions about his family. He was suspended for six months and confined to his monastery in Mexico City.

All the sentences having been read, one of the bishops rose to his feet and delivered a lengthy sermon on the "one and only true faith." After heaping a tirade of humiliating insults upon the penitents, he ordered them to kneel. "Do you hereby pledge your eternal allegiance and obedience to the Pope and belief in the dogma of faith?"

In unison, all answered, "Yes, I believe."

The bishop continued with a recitation of the prohibitions against them for the rest of their lives and the lives of their progeny for three generations to come. "We disable you from holding public office or one of honor, nor may you wear on your person gold, silver, pearls, or precious stones, nor silk camelot, nor fine cloth, nor go on horseback, nor carry arms nor exercise or use any of the other things which by common right, laws and pragmatics of these Kingdoms and Instructions of the Holy Office of the Inquisition are prohibited to those similarly disabled."

Following this was a sequence of threats and descriptions of the hell and damnation that awaited those who relapsed and returned to their evil way of life, sinning against the Church. "All who return to the beliefs of the Old Religion are condemned to eternal darkness," warned the bishop.

The only concern of Luis', at that moment, was that their lives had been spared and where there is life, God Almighty will provide!

That night, Alonso de Peralta enjoyed some of his finest wine. He saluted the conversion of Luis de Carvajal and his family. A personal triumph, in some respects. He would succeed in destroying the legend surrounding Luis by destroying the image of the man.

In his cell that night, Luis spent hours in prayer, entreating God to forgive him for what must appear to be a betrayal. "Lord, do not forsake Thy servant, for what I attested to as a willingness to abjure before my torturers were lies offered only in the hope of saving my life and the lives of my loved ones. I have done this so I may continue to work in Thy glory and in praise of Thy name when we leave this despicable place. Adonai have mercy upon us. Amen."

CHAPTER XI

INTERVENTION AND INTOXICATION

Leonor's husband, Jorge de Almeida, was of medium stature, with a swarthy complexion. The scar on his left cheek was a souvenir from an escapade on the high seas, when his vessel encountered one of the English corsairs which regularly plundered the waters near New Spain. Jorge was not only rugged and fearless but was a successful businessman as well. His enterprising nature had earned him an important place in the community. Even though he and Leonor were Secret Jews, he was careful to maintain the semblance of that of a pious Catholic. He attended church regularly and belonged to several Christian organizations. His fine reputation deflected the slightest suspicion.

When he learned that the Inquisition had dispatched Francisca and her daughters to different convents to serve their time, he went before the Holy Office to request that the women be reconciled in a private house to do their penance, under his supervision. The Holy Office agreed to the plan and the de Carvajal women were placed in a residence within the proximity of the Indian Market in Santiago Tlatelolco, close to the Franciscan monastery. A friendly old friar, Fray Pedro de Oroz, was assigned to visit them every day to instruct them in Catholic doctrine and to hear confession.

Francisca and the girls were overjoyed at their reunion. They all profusely expressed their thanks to Jorge and Leonor gave him a tender kiss, exclaiming, "My husband, you are formidable!"

Luis, however, did not fare well in his assignment to the Hospital de los Convalescientes of San Hipolito. Brother Matthew Garcia was to minister to his spiritual needs and Larias de Valdes, the official prison warden, was to supervise Luis' compliance with services to be performed. The inquisitors were convinced that Luis would prove himself a dedicated and devoted Christian.

The hospital, a large complex, was a convalescent home for the elderly and the infirm. Luis was given the most menial jobs to do and although he quietly went about his chores, inwardly he seethed. *Not to worry,* he reflected. *This is my first step to freedom; my first step to resuming my life as a Jew.*

Jorge realized that he must seek some relief for the family — a pardon of sorts — so that they would not remain in their penitential cloaks, nor imprisoned in places designated by the Holy Office for the balance of their sentences. So, once again, he appeared before the inquisitors with a suggestion. "Your excellencies, my business activities demand that I return to Spain. I must escort and supervise an important shipment of silver, jewels, and commodities. As you know, I am one of the chief importers-exporters for this region. My contract with the Royal House requires my immediate supervision of any such consignments between Spain and her colonies. Because I am most experienced and familiar with the needs of both the Church and the army, as well as the general population, I must conduct transactions personally." Jorge winked broadly and added, "This trip is particularly important because I shall deliver the Royal 'one-fifth' to the Court. It is a sizable amount."

Their excellencies agreed that he must see to his responsibilities and thanked him. "You are to be commended for your fine work on behalf of their Majesties and Mother Church. Is there anything else you wish to bring to our attention?"

Already they are counting their share of the profits, thought Jorge. *The dogs are almost salivating.* Aloud he said, "One thing more, Sirs. I respectfully request that my brother-in-law Luis de Carvajal be permitted to stay with his mother and sisters while I am away, so they may have companionship and male supervision."

The Holy Office acquiesced and indicated that Luis would be released from his assignment at the San Hipolito hospital. One of the inquisitors said, "Fray Pedro has spoken highly of your Luis and is impressed with his language abilities. Upon his recommendation, Luis will be assigned as a teacher of Indian children and as personal scribe to the Fray at the Colegia de Santa Cruz (Holy Cross Academy). It is not far from the family. He will serve all day at the Colegia and return to the family in the evening. If all goes well with this arrangement, he may be permitted longer intervals of time at home." He concluded with, "In the name of the Lord Jesus Christ, we wish you Godspeed."

Jorge could not get over his good fortune. They had agreed to his requests. He was careful to mask his surprise and elation as he bowed and bade them farewell. There was no time to be lost. Preparations for his ship's departure must be made at once. But first he hurried off to tell Francisca and the girls what had transpired and then to the hospital where Luis greeted the news with tears of joy.

When Luis rejoined the family, he found that they had strayed somewhat from their secret observances. This was understandable, considering the circumstances. It was difficult to avoid certain foods or to observe fast days with Fray Pedro visiting them on a daily basis. The Fray was fond of the de Carvajals and soon Luis became his favorite. They worked together closely at the Colegia, where Luis enjoyed many privileges.

It was not long before he restored the observances and practicies of Judaism in the house. Soon they were spending evenings with invited friends who often joined them behind locked doors in prayer. The organized clandestine meetings were held at the de Carvajal house or in Pachuca, in Manuel de Lucena's house. The Lucena's lived just outside of Mexico City.

With more freedom of movement and privacy granted by the Fray, Luis was able to visit with other families who welcomed his preaching. His reputation spread among Secret Jews. He was held in high esteem as a teacher and zealot and great leader.

One Friday evening in March of 1591, when Luis was conducting a prayer meeting at home, his friend Manuel de Lucena arrived a little late — but with a good excuse. He had with him a young lady and her mother whom he wished to introduce to the group. Luis, who was about to reprimand him, quickly refrained. Instead, he embraced Manuel and welcomed his guests.

Manuel made the introductions. "This is Clara Enriquez and her daughter, Justa Mendez, whose father was the late Francisco Mendez."

Everyone offered a greeting. Justa smiled demurely and then placed her hand in Luis' as though it was the most natural thing to do, as though she had been doing it all her life. She was immediately smitten with this handsome, charismatic youth and her heart told her she would follow him wherever he led.

As for Luis, he thought he was having another vision. As her hand lingered in his, he observed that surely she must be the most beautiful of all Jewesses. He was captivated and the moment renewed deep, stirring passions he had not dealt with for some time.

The girl was nothing short of spectacular. Nineteen years old, Justa possessed exceptional physical qualities. It was no wonder that friends and relatives referred to her as "la hermosa" — the beautiful. She was tall and slender. Her young, firm breasts and wasp-waist curved gracefully into lean hips. Delicately sculptured and glowing, her face was framed by raven, silken tresses worn in a chignon. The almond-shaped eyes, a startling cornflower blue, held Luis' with an intensity that made him catch his breath.

She was dressed in her Sabbath finery — a lovely, flowing dress of vermillion velvet was simply adorned by soft lace at the throat, complemented by a delicate brooch. Suspended from her dainty ears were pearl drop earrings.

Luis stood there, with her hand in his, feeling somewhat awkward. She leaned toward him and softly whispered, "Luis, I shall stay by your side always." Then, again, her sensuous lips mouthed the word, "Always."

In that miniscule span of time, Luis experienced an epiphany. The Almighty had sent him someone to love. Someone to share his life's work. The Lord had blessed His servant with wondrous gifts.

It was an enchanted night. Luis conducted the prayers and hymns; he even recited original works. Justa sat there mesmerized, her gaze never leaving his face. Well read and bright, she was able to participate in much of the devotional service. This was a source of much pleasure to Luis.

After the meeting, Francisca served refreshments. The ardent attraction between Justa and Luis was palpable, not only to themselves but to all around the table. The men teased, "Luis, look around. We are here, too. Will you not grace us with a nod of your head now and then?" and "Justa, your face will freeze with that puppy-dog look if you do not change your expression."

Finally, Luis responded by saying to Justa, "Ignore these old ones. They have forgotten what it is to be young and in the company of a goddess."

The blush that spread across Justa's face would have made a rose look blanched and faded. Everyone laughed good-naturedly and the conversation went back to matters at hand. Francisca, however, now had an agenda in mind, so she made her way around the table to position herself next to Justa.

"Dear girl, soon we will celebrate the Feast of Pascua. Will you give us the pleasure of your company at the seder? Perhaps you would like to spend the week with us?"

A radiant Justa answered, "I shall be only too happy to be your guest and," she added quickly, "I am sure my mother will approve." She was over-joyed at the invitation, but would her mother really approve? Francisca's next comment solved the problem.

"Both you and your mother are invited to join us and we shall observe the holiday together," Francisca offered. *It was only proper, after all*, she thought.

Luis beamed.

The following Sunday, usually spent visiting neighbors and family, Luis asked his mother to accompany him on the short trip to Clara Enriquez' house so that he might visit with Justa. Francisca kissed her son resoundingly on the cheek, uttering words of approval.

Clara welcomed them with open arms and immediately put the kettle on for tea. "Justa will be back shortly," she explained, when Luis questioned her whereabouts. "I sent her on an errand. Meanwhile, let us enjoy a cup of tea and a chat."

Luis paced up and down, barely tolerating what seemed to be a long wait. Francisca and Clara smiled and nodded to each other. Finally, the door opened and an exuberant Justa entered. She was dressed more sedately than on Friday evening but was just as radiant. Minding her manners, she greeted Francisca first, kissed her mother and then turned to Luis. He took her hand in his and kissed it. Justa brazenly kissed him on the cheek. Fearful that her mother disapproved of her impetuous action, she grinned sheepishly at the two women, silently begging for approval.

When the elders burst into laughter, Justa giggled and sighed with relief. The four of them were swept up in the magic of the moment. Forgotten was the Inquisition, the sanbenitos, the sentences not yet commuted. Love filled the room and enveloped them in a warm embrace. Suddenly transported into another dimension, there was a semblance of normalcy pervading. Life was the way it was supposed to be. The future seemed to hold promise. The madness was behind them.

That Passover was a joyous one for the family. There was so much for which to be thankful. They were together again and soon, with the Almighty's help, their sentences would be lifted. Their new friends, Clara and Justa, joined them and their other guests in the celebration.

A frenzy of preparation had taken place days in advance. The house was meticulously scrubbed, guest quarters were refreshed with new linens and articles of comfort. Francisca and her daughters baked tortillas and cooked fish. Luis had the job of securing a little white lamb to be roasted according to the tradition taught him by his father. Vegetables and fruits were attractively laid out on platters. He watched lovingly as his mother and sisters went about their chores. *Good women*, he thought, *who will surely have a place in the Kingdom of Heaven.*

Everything was in readiness by the time the guests began arriving in the late afternoon before sundown after which the Seder would begin. Justa and her mother contributed some prepared delicacies; in particular were some apple fritters Justa had baked especially for Luis. From the moment she arrived, she remained at his side. The elders were amused to see how she followed him about and quick to notice how much Luis enjoyed it.

At the Seder table, she sat to his left and his mother to his right. Luis' sisters and guests were interspersed around the large, bountiful table. The wonderful meal was coupled with an unforgettable Passover service. Luis, in eloquent terms, recited the meaning and the history of the Passover observance. He was mesmerizing. As the story unfolded, everyone felt a sense of excitement and commitment. The young narrator was truly a man of dedication and his enthusiasm inspired his audience. Admiration and love for Luis poured forth from his listeners as he recited some of his poetry. Justa sat quietly, nodding occasionally and smiling. The celebration ended with a prayer for God's miraculous redemption and their return to the Promised Land upon the coming of the Messiah. Everyone congratulated Luis.

The emotion that flooded Justa's being was evident by the tears in her eyes as she put her hand in Luis'. "You are wonderful, *mi amor*, so brilliant, so impressive. You are a born leader," Justa told him and sniffed daintily into her handkerchief.

"Justa, hermosa, you will make me blush with your compliments. I thank you for your moving words." Luis did not know how to handle this impetuous girl.

Suddenly, Justa said to Luis, "It is so lovely tonight. May we go for a stroll?" She was all smiles.

Luis asked Clara and his mother if they might be excused for a little while. Both mothers encouraged them to "go and enjoy the fresh air of the evening." Francisca gave her son a playful little pat on his backside, warning him jokingly, "Behave yourself as a gentleman. Do not besmirch the good name of de Carvajal men."

He kissed his mother, saying, "I have never let you down. Do not frighten Justa. She will think I am a big ogre in disguise." They all laughed.

Justa flashed him an irresistible smile. "You are my handsome and brave conquistador, my hero, like the honored heroes of the Bible."

He fetched her mantilla, placed it around her shoulders and led her out the door into a perfect night, a night that was crystal clear, softly illuminated by a crescent moon. A comfortable breeze danced about caressingly. The streets were deserted, for the hour was late. From a nearby house came the sounds of a love song softly played on a guitar. They walked slowly, humming the tune, not speaking but experiencing and sharing that first-time sensation of being totally in love and the overwhelming desire to touch and feel and consume.

As if on cue, they turned to face each other. Justa's breath caught in her throat as she uttered a little cry. Luis drew her to him and tilted her lovely face upward to kiss her gently at first, and then passionately. They stood there holding each other, their bodies trembling. "I love you, beautiful Justa, and from this day forever shall I look after you and protect you."

She could barely respond. A solitary tear slipped down her cheek as she whispered, "Forever, Luis. Forever, mi corazon."

Justa and Luis spent much time together. She often visited him at the Colegia, sometimes accompanied by friends. Soon, it became a matter of routine. They engaged in stimulating theological conversations and exchanged ideas. Luis was highly informative relating much of what he read in Fray Pedro's library, where he had available to him Greek and Latin classics, bibles, and books of devotion. He was particularly impressed with the writings of the Dominican priest, Jerome Oleaster. It was amazing, he told his friends, how reminiscent the priest's Thirteen Articles of the Faith were of Judaic religious principles. During their discussions at the Colegia, they were extremely careful, often using cryptic terms and double entendres, just in case someone uninvited should appear. Luis wondered, from time to time, whether the friar suspected anything.

The hours which Justa and Luis spent alone were happy ones filled with expressions of love and hopes for the future. "When our sentences are lifted and we are free to travel, Justa dearest, you and your mother shall join my family in going to a land where we can worship Adonai freely."

"Oh, Luis, my heart is so full of hope for us. Will we ever really escape from this hell?"

Hugging her, he kissed her tenderly on the forehead. "*Si, mi amor, si.* Just wait. Have patience and faith. There are good days ahead."

She tilted her head and looked at him longingly, saying softly, "On the lips, Luis, on the lips."

Luis was most accommodating.

In the fall of 1592, to demonstrate his affection for her, he prepared a special little book as a gift on the Great Day, Yom Kippur. In it were his favorite prayers and some of his own compositions and he inscribed it to her with words of deep affection.

"Oh, Luis, you are such a love to create this wonderful gift for me. I shall always treasure it."

He kissed her and advised, "Keep it hidden, my darling. Be careful that you do not put us in harm's way through carelessness."

"Beloved, this is a symbol of your feelings for me. I shall guard it dearly and never permit it to be evidence for the 'devils'."

Several months later, while on their way to visit friends for an evening of prayer, she told Luis, "I have your little book with me tucked away near my bosom." She blushed. "I do so want to show it to our friends."

"Be careful, my sweet, that you do not drop it."

She smiled warmly. "It is most safe nestled near my heart. Do not fear, dearest."

When they arrived, their friends greeted them enthusiastically. An evening with Luis was always an inspiration. After some polite conversation, a discussion of theological concepts ensued while they enjoyed coffee and small cakes. Justa, anxious to display her treasure and to read from it, exclaimed, "I must show you what Luis has created for me. I have hidden it here in my clothing, it is so precious." She turned away and reached under her jacket to retrieve the velvet-covered notebook. The others discreetly looked away.

"Luis!" her shriek pierced the air. "It is gone. Oh, my God, it is gone. What have I done?"

He was at her side in an instant, not displaying the panic he felt. "We must retrace our steps at once. Do not fear, my dear one, we shall find it."

Everyone in that room knew what would happen if the book fell into the wrong hands.

Justa was crying. "How foolish am I? I just wanted to keep it near my heart...I meant no harm...and now that is exactly what I have caused..."

Luis quieted her and wiped away her tears. "Come, come — it will be fine. We shall find the book." He turned to his friends. "Regrettably, we must leave you."

Out on the street, not wishing to attract unnecessary attention, they walked as nonchalantly as they could, all the while scanning every inch of the path which they had taken before. As they passed the local bakery, a faint sound attracted them — the whisper of a name. Dared they turn? It sounded like someone had softly called, "Luis, aca, aca, look here."

The frightened pair turned slowly and there in the doorway stood the baker, beckoning to them. They recognized him as one who occasionally attended prayer meetings at Luis' house. He beckoned them to follow him into the store. Once inside, he pulled them aside out of view of the window. "I believe I have something you are missing. I know this because I recognized the names in it." He held up the little book.

Justa leapt at it and clutched it lovingly to her. "Oh, Senor, how can I ever thank you? I thought it was lost forever and, far worse, that it may have been found by someone from the Holy Office. I cannot thank you enough." Impulsively, she hugged her benefactor who blushed profusely as a wide grin spread across his beefy face.

Luis echoed her sentiments. "Yes, my friend, *muchos gracias*." He, too, was so grateful he could have kissed the baker himself but opted for shaking his hand instead.

The baker, a romantic at heart, insisted they take with them a bag of rolls and some tasty cookies. He enjoyed seeing people in love and smiled benevolently as the two happily departed, munching on some of the sweets.

Luis never expressed the fear that had gripped him that night. Anticipating the worst scenario, his mind had raced to various possibilities should the book have fallen into the hands of the Inquisition. The family would have had to escape — a difficult prospect. He had even considered familial suicide but had discarded the idea — suicides lose their souls, and thus their chance for salvation.

He cringed at the thought of what might have happened had not the baker found the prized possession.

CHAPTER XII

FORTUNE AND FLIGHT

When Luis' brothers, Baltasar and Miguel, escaped from Mexico, they made their way from Rome to Pisa, where they settled. Jorge ascertained their whereabouts when he arrived in Madrid and traveled to see them. He brought with him letters from Luis telling his brothers of his visions and of God's message to him. Luis signed his letters with the name, Joseph Lumbroso, which he explained came about because he believed that the Lord had enlightened him and chosen him to bring "light"to his brethren. "Change your names, as well," he urged.

The brothers cried with happiness when they read the letters. They kissed the pages and Baltasar declared, "We shall indeed change our names, dear brother." The letters they wrote in return affirmed that Baltasar would be known as David, and Miguel, as Jacob Lumbroso.

"I am now married," Baltasar happily wrote, "and Miguel is studying medicine. We are living freely as Jews here in Pisa. It is our wish that we shall see you and the family here soon."

Jorge explained to them that he was not returning to Mexico as yet but that he would arrange for the delivery of the letters through friends returning with the spring flota.

The next few days were spent catching up on all that had transpired in Mexico City: the arrests, the trials, the sentences. Jorge regretted that he could only share a brief visit with his brothers-in-law but he was anxious to get back to Madrid, where the family still had sympathizers in high places who had a deep respect for the de Carvajals.

Once back in Madrid, Jorge went to see some of his Old Christian and New Christian friends. A distant cousin with whom he was lodging, told him that before Baltasar left Spain for Italy he had approached the Secretary of the Supreme Council of the Inquisition and the secretary of the Indies. "It seems that there was a question of a large sum of money to buy the freedom for the family. Poor Baltasar — he was not able to meet the price, not even just for Luis."

Jorge interjected, "If it is the money, that is not a problem. I can be of great help. I have funds. The plight of the family must be presented before the

Supreme Council and a request that their "penances" be withdrawn and that they be released from mandatory housing."

His host offered, "We shall intercede because of the admiration we have for the de Carvajals. It will not be easy, you know. Meanwhile, go about your business. We shall do the best we can." He embraced Jorge. "Buena suerta. Good luck."

Jorge shook his hand. "I shall not forget this. Thank you with all my heart."

His next stop was the warehouses to oversee the completion of orders for foodstuffs, fabrics, military wares and dozens of household items to be transported to his ship waiting at the Port of Seville. For the next several months, he continued to pressure his liaisons regarding the family and he continued to wait. Finally, word came. A hearing had been arranged.

Jorge diligently presented his case before the Council. When he concluded his plea, he was advised that the matter would be taken under consideration. In the interim, they proposed a plan for the required "ransom" for the family's releases. Jorge was taken aback by the exorbitant price of redemption which they demanded, but he offered them an extravagant sum from his personal account.

"It is not enough," the Council advised him. "However, we shall give you the opportunity to raise the additional money through letters addressed to various ecclesiastics and monasteries in Mexico, urging them to contribute alms. Give these letters to Luis de Carvajal, *el Mozo*, so that he can accumulate these funds."

Jorge did not show his surprise at this gesture of cooperation. "I am most grateful, Sirs, for your kind help. I should be ready to sail when the fleet leaves from Seville within a fortnight." Bowing respectfully, he took his leave, hardly able to suppress the exhilaration he felt.

The Council's reflection on the matter was that a man like Jorge de Almeida who brought a large share of wealth to the kingdom had to be compensated somehow.

When Luis heard that his brother-in-law had returned to Mexico, he rushed to see him.

"Ah, Luis, I was planning to see you but you are too fast for me," Jorge said.

They embraced and Luis asked for news, which he hungrily absorbed. To know that his brothers were alive and well made him ecstatic. When Jorge told him about the letters of recommendation to raise money for their releases, he could not contain his joy. It would take 820 pesos, in addition to the sum Jorge offered, for the Royal Court to issue a decree of rehabilitation and freedom. The men decided this would not be a problem.

Luis went to his mother's house that evening to tell them all the good tidings. Francisca, who had been ailing for awhile, was so happy. "This is my cure sent by Adonai. I am better already," the grateful woman declared. She kissed Luis and embraced her daughters. "Let us pray together for better days ahead. 'Almighty God, aid of all souls...'" she began and all joined in.

Later, Luis said encouragingly, "I am sure, my loved ones, that our lives will improve when the matter of our freedom is completed, and that will be when I have secured the 'ransom'. I must go to Fray Pedro in the morning to ask for permission to travel to the monasteries in order to raise the money." Hope was a welcome sedative. All slept soundly that night.

Luis had a concern about leaving the colegia at that particular time because he had not yet completed an assignment given him by a visiting prelate. As he lay upon his bed that night, he reminisced about the turn of events in connection with the assignment. The whole thing had started under peculiar circumstances. One day, Fray Pedro was visited by a commissary of the Inquisition. Luis had observed them as they stood talking at the end of the hallway. Every once in a while, they had glanced his way and then continued conversing in soft tones, completely inaudible to Luis. He remembered how uneasy he had felt. When the visitor approached him and requested a sample of his handwriting, Luis was fearful. Complying with the request, he wondered if they had found some of his poems or compositions, or perhaps the notes he had taken from books in the Fray's library.

What relief he had felt when the commissary exclaimed, "Bueno! Fray Pedro told me you have an excellent hand. There are some papers which I shall require you to copy for me. It is a dissertation written by a local priest."

"I shall begin immediately, sir," Luis had responded. Another deliverance.

Now, at the present time, urged by Jorge to go about the task of collecting alms, completing the writing assignment presented a problem. *Perhaps,* Luis thought, *I can give the balance of the work to a few of my best Indian pupils. He would go to the Fray with this suggestion in the morning. Time was of the essence.*

The next day when he presented his idea to the Fray, much to Luis' surprise, Fray Pedro was most annoyed. "I do not like it that you would desert work assigned to you."

His reaction stunned Luis inasmuch as their relationship was a congenial one. "Padre, the Court will not permit too much time to elapse," Luis told him. "I must act quickly. There are several scribes whom I am willing to pay personally to do the work, if the commissary consents to this arrangement."

Mumbling under his breath, Fray Pedro turned and walked away.

Disconsolate, Luis returned to his desk. "Your servant needs your help, Lord," he softly entreated.

Later that day, a solution suddenly presented itself which satisfied everyone and enabled Luis to begin his "pilgrimage", free of any guilt feelings. The priest who had authored the dissertation asked for its return because he had been assigned to another city. The commissary had no choice but to discontinue the copy work. Luis sighed with relief. Fray Pedro regarded the coincidence as an indication of God's will. "Come, Luis, we must set about getting more letters of support for your mission. I shall advise the Franciscan and Dominican monks to assist you. We shall even request the aid of the viceroy." He seemed so eager to help. Luis could not believe his good fortune.

After Jorge had been home for a few months, he got word through close friends that the Inquisition was showing a lot of interest in his activities and holdings and also those of his brother-in-law, Antonio de Caceres, Catalina's husband. He decided to move about warily to determine just how interested they were. As a precaution, he transferred money and the ownership of his hacienda to his uncle, Tomas de Fonseca. He set about to collect debts and to liquidate assets. He realized that his dream of remaining in Mexico might become a nightmare.

Early one morning, while he was enjoying his coffee and a light breakfast of biscuits and jelly, there was a loud, ominous knock at the door. Jorge rushed to a window and drew the curtain slightly aside, just enough for him to view the visitor. He recognized the man as a messenger from the Holy Office. This was one door he would not open. Instead, he grabbed the pouch he had prepared for such a possibility and ran out the back entrance of the house. His horse, ever ready, carried him at a quick pace over the road to Taxco.

It did not take long for the Inquisitorial office to determine that Jorge had fled and to surmise, logically, that he could be found in Taxco where he owned mines and property and a large contingent of natives under his stewardship. An emissary of the Holy Office, Luis Movan, came to Taxco with orders for Jorge's arrest. However, a strange, miraculous intervention occurred. Not too far from Taxco there was an arena wherein many bulls were housed. It was unusual that the day Movan arrived, a bull had escaped from its pen. Even more unusual, this bull had made its way to the exact spot in front of the government's mining office where Movan now stood contemplating his next move. The move he made was not the one he had anticipated. The bull attacked him so viciously that the unfortunate victim died almost instantly.

Grateful for the reprieve, Jorge made more arrangements for the transfer of holdings and money to his older brother, who would remain. Jorge and his younger brother Ricardo had already decided to go into hiding until they could leave.

Rodriquez de Silva had déjà vu when he was awakened by a soft knocking and equally as soft voices identifying themselves at his door. When the two men entered, he threw his arms around them, as he had done some time ago with Baltasar and Miguel.

"Welcome, Jorge. Welcome, Ricardo. Come in, my dear friends." He kissed them on both cheeks. "Tell me all. What brings you here?"

Jorge recounted the recent chain of events and then asked, "Will you permit us to stay until we decide what course of action we must take?"

Rodriquez assured them, "Mi amigos, this is your home for as long as you need it."

The men spent many hours making plans and discussing alternatives. Finally, they agreed that they must escape to Spain. "Once in Spain," Jorge said, "I can continue to fight for the de Carvajals and also clear my own name, if necessary. I will go to Rome to make an appeal, if I have to. You know, the Papacy there does not share the same ideas with the Inquisition of the Iberian Peninsula. They have extended a welcome and helping hand to Spanish and Portugese Judaizers."

Rodriquez agreed, "I hear that is true, my friend, and certainly a good idea worth pursuing."

Jorge continued, "I have devoted friends in Spain who will continue to exert their influence. In fact, one of my most trusted amigos is the secretary to the Cardinal."

Rodriquez was impressed. He blurted out, "Jorge, I wish to throw in my lot with yours. May I join you?"

"Of course, of course. Wonderful!" was the response.

During the next forty-eight hours, Rodriquez secured whatever money and assets he could take with him and designated the rest of his estate to relatives who would act on his behalf. "Jorge, I have a cousin who is the captain of a vessel at the Port of Vera Cruz, who is one of us. In fact, he is the one who helped Baltasar and Miguel. I am positive we can obtain passage on his ship. He sails for Spain in the flota at the end of the month. We can get there with time to spare if we leave by morning and, I am sure, he will sequester us until sailing time."

"Bueno, well done. Let us get some sleep and then make ready to leave before daylight," Jorge suggested.

Under a still dark sky, barely streaked with streamers of nebulous white, the three riders made their way to the Port of Vera Cruz. The terrain was difficult. The men and their horses were plagued by mosquitoes and other insects. The air was sultry and sweltering and they were thankful for the occasional stream where they could refresh themselves. As they made their way to the coast and then down along the coastline to Vera Cruz, they progressed slowly, stopping now and then for a meal and a night's lodging. After several days, they arrived at the Port and located Rodriquez' cousin. The captain received them warmly and showed them to their quarters aboard ship.

The trio remained as inconspicuous as possible, counting the hours as each day passed until, at last, they heard the command to set sail.

CHAPTER XIII

THE REPRIEVE

Luis' other brother-in-law, Antonio, was as wily and adventurous as he was handsome. But now he was in trouble again. He kissed his wife Catalina, and their daughter Leonor and said a hurried but tearful "*adios*." Catalina understood his decision to leave. The authorities were searching for him. A warrant had been issued for his arrest based on reports from vendors that he had sold them damaged goods. This scenario was not a new one for Antonio. He had been apprehended on several occasions with these charges pending against him. Somehow, he had always eluded imprisonment, particularly because he was capable of meeting any fines that were imposed.

Before he decided to leave, he gave a considerable sum of money to his lawyer, advising him, "Settle these claims as swiftly as possible so that I may go on a business trip to the Orient. You must buy back my good reputation, Senor." They both laughed.

His lawyer assured him, "Do not worry. I shall handle the matter most expeditiously."

Much money exchanged hands and Antonio obtained his papers to sail. As he was handed his permits, the attorney smiled and shook Antonio's hand. "You see, I told you to have no fear. It is done. Good fortune, amigo."

The fear of not obtaining the sailing permits was not the only concern of Antonio's. Recently, he had received a warning from close friends that the Inquisition was displaying an inordinate interest in his holdings and also those of Catalina. He knew that Jorge had already left the country. Urgency begot action. He had prepared for such an exigency by arranging for the transfer of his holdings to close associates and relatives.

A hasty, tearful goodbye to the family caused him much grief the night he planned to leave. He tore himself from his wife's arms as she said, sorrowfully, "Go in God's good graces, my love."

Antonio went directly to the house of his friend Roberto Perez, who was waiting in preparation to join him in the hard ride to Vera Cruz. They planned to take this route rather than go to Acapulco because it would take them to the port in time to join the upcoming voyage to the Orient of the Armada of the South Seas.

The seaport at Vera Cruz bustled with captains and crews preparing for the long journey. Cargoes of supplies were being loaded on the participating vessels. One of them was the seven-hundred-ton galleon, the Nuestra Senora de la Concepcion, owned by Antonio. "I desperately hope, Roberto, that we shall make it out of the harbor before a possible official order from the Holy Office can reach us to impound the ship and arrest me," Antonio said anxiously.

"But do you know for sure that they intend to do this?" asked Roberto.

"They came for Jorge. How much longer before they come for me?" Antonio asked.

The two men huddled in a corner of the wharf, watching the activity. The day slowly surrendered to the night. Low-flying clouds lent an eerie murkiness to the failing daylight. The sky's deepening hues of charcoal and violet conspired to obliterate the glow of the moon.

"So, my friend, all goes well, eh?" Roberto slapped Antonio on the back. "By this time tomorrow, we shall be well on our way."

"May God so will it. Roberto, are you sure of the trustworthiness of this Captain Machado?"

"Rest assured, amigo. I am a personal friend of this captain and the crew has sailed with him before. They are devoted to him."

"Bueno, Roberto, but does Machado understand that I shall take charge when we break away from the flota in Panama City?"

"Yes. I have explained that to him and also have given him your promise to buy him another command at the Port of Panama. It is muy importante that you keep this promise, so that he will keep his to escort your ship to Manila."

"Of course," agreed Antonio. "Did you warn him of the danger? This is a big gamble for us all. The Philippines are not friendly to Spanish ships and there are always the Asian pirates with whom to contend." He sighed. "Since the Portugese were granted de facto control of the Islands and the trade routes, they treat us as if we were pirates. I am depending upon my connections there for our safety."

"God's blessing — and *mucho dinero* — should take care of that." Roberto suppressed a nervous little laugh. Jumping to his feet, he whispered, "Come, it is dark enough now. They have finished loading and the captain has just given the signal that it is safe for us to come forward. Let us join the people on line waiting to board."

Slinging his knapsack over his shoulder, Antonio quickly pressed fingers to his midriff. *Yes, the most important "cargo" was well hidden inside his bulky tunic.* The thought evoked a smile of confidence.

The change of command at Panama City took a bit of explaining to the crew but, with a promise of extra compensation at the end of the trip, the men were cooperative. Antonio sighed with relief. He had not looked forward to this trip. There were many problems. Because of its size, his ship had to anchor at Perico, six miles westward of the port, which was located on the Pacific side of the Isthmus. Its waters were extremely shallow. Some of the cargo from the Nuestra Senora, unloaded at Perico, would have to be transported by smaller vessels to the port, where Antonio intended to sell many colonial-made items to traders from nearby territories. The plan was to continue then to Manila where he would avail himself of the exotic and luxurious wares offered there. His mouth watered at the thought of how much profit he would make. Antonio realized that everything rested upon his return to Mexico without the threat of arrest.

"Ay, Roberto, how I hate this torrid, unhealthy climate."

"Si, but we have no choice. This is the path we must take, for sure," Roberto answered.

The two men sat and chatted about home and their families, how they missed their wives and children. They watched as the crew unloaded some of the merchandise for transactions at the Port. The *cochineal*, a popular red dye, would bring a handsome price. Almost exclusive to production in Mexico, it was in great demand elsewhere in the area and abroad.

Antonio reminisced, "Roberto, old friend, I cannot help but think about the last trip we made to Seville. That was a rough one!"

"Rough, yes, but we outran those 'corsarios' and gave them a good fight, to boot. *Dios mio*, you fought like a lion! Everyone was impressed — even the French corsairs, no doubt. They went running like a pack of beaten dogs, with their tails tucked under."

As a true swashbuckler at heart, Antonio loved the excitement of the sea. With corsairs roaming the Spanish Lake, encounters were not uncommon. "Well, let us hope that we will do as well against any Asian pirates, if we run across their path."

"Not to worry. You are the '*El Drague*' of the Spanish fleet, just as Senor Francis Drake of the English corsairs was called. He is their 'drague;' you are ours."

The business at Panama completed, the Nuestra Senora de la Concepcion turned her bow westward to the vast waters of the Pacific. Not too far behind was the Santa Ana Maria, commanded by Capt. Machado. Antonio's ship had left Panama a few days earlier than the fleet in order to get a vantage point in Manila. It would have been safer traveling with the other ships but he decided to take his chances, with the Santa Ana Maria not too far behind. "The early bird catches the worm," he observed.

Surprisingly, the voyage was relatively uneventful except for the appearance of a few armed caravels that made no effort to engage the two large ships. Antonio remarked, "They know they are outclassed and are wise to permit us to go undisturbed."

Roberto agreed. "The little pipsqueaks! We could squash them in a minute." They both laughed. Roberto continued, "You were wise to anticipate such emergencies and to secure this well-equipped galleon. Those *corsarios* will not have the nerve to challenge us."

Antonio turned to him with a mischievous smile on his face. "You know what, my friend, let us fire a volley at them anyway, just for the fun of it."

The winds were favorable and after almost six weeks the call of "Land ho!" was heard from the crow's nest atop the main mast. Cheers of excitement greeted the call — land, at last! — a chance to stretch 'sea legs' and enjoy a little relaxation in the form of liquor and female companionship. The trip had been a tedious one and the men had grown restless. Having reached the Port of Manila, they were now all smiles. The captain congratulated them on a job well done.

They had agreed that the Nuestra Senora would pull into the harbor, while the Santa Ana Maria would remain out a ways. "Just a precautionary measure," explained Antonio. "After I present my papers and we receive clearance, I will signal for you to bring your ship alongside. Remember, do not move in until I give the sign. I am not certain of my reception at the port."

The plan was for Antonio and two of his officers to go ashore and present themselves to the proper authorities. Antonio was depending on his lawyer's assurances that everything was in order. As he stood before the officer-in-charge, he had the strangest feeling that something had gone awry. Within moments, he and his men were in chains. He protested loudly, demanding an explanation, but to no avail. The three were thrown into a jail cell.

Meanwhile, Roberto waited for a signal to heave-to and make landfall. He, in turn, was to hoist the banner to signal the Santa Ana Maria to do likewise. Antonio had cautioned him before he left, "If I do not signal, you will position yourself in such a way that you can defend the ship against all boarders." Now Roberto's worst fears were becoming a reality. He suspected, correctly, that if they had arrested Antonio and his men, then boarding the ship and confiscating everything would be the next move. After waiting the specified time for a signal and none forthcoming, Roberto ordered the crew to maneuver the ship into a defensive position.

Several hours passed. Nothing transpired. It was now time to put the second plan into operation. After dark, Roberto sent four of his men in a small boat to the shore. Their mission was to locate Antonio and the others.

There was so much hustle and bustle at the Port of Manila that the activity of the four sailors went unnoticed. They hid their small dinghy in a cove and went ashore. Moving stealthily and swiftly, they soon located the jail where they observed Antonio and his two officers being held. The four men moved in expeditiously and noiselessly. Two guards were on duty. Their throats were slit before they even sensed the presence of the interlopers. Keys were confiscated, cell doors flung open and seven men slipped away into the dark night.

Aboard the Nuestra Senora there was much celebration, though short-lived. Antonio ordered, "Prepare to set sail before dawn for the Port of Macao." Two previous trips to the Orient had acquainted Antonio with the area and its potential as a source of fine goods. Once there, he hoped, things would go easily. They escaped the Manila harbor with no incident and headed out to the South China Sea.

"Tell me, Antonio, what happened back there? Why did they arrest you? I thought it had all been arranged —"

"Arranged! Ha! Yes, it had been arranged but how could we anticipate what would happen at the other end?" He threw his arms up in frustration. "Who could foretell that the authority I was to report to would turn out to be the one I had a run-in with last year — some little matter about defective goods and contraband. Well, I bought my way out of that problem and I believed it to be past history. Today, of all the bad luck, that same scoundrel was on duty. The *bastardo* was just waiting to get his pound of flesh. But, we fixed him good, eh, Roberto?"

The charges levied against Antonio were not totally unfounded. It was not unusual for trading ships to deal in smuggled goods and to engage in secret trade with European merchant ships. Even though a large portion of a ship's profit was sent to the Spanish Court, a significant amount of merchandise changed hands during the local trading. Many a ship's captain was in danger of being charged with contraband. Several times in the past, Antonio had faced such charges. Fortunately, his connections and funds were such that he always escaped incarceration.

On this trip, his ship carried not only the desirable cochineal and other products produced in New Spain but also European items in great demand, such as wine, cloth, and olive oil. Most importantly, he carried a large amount of gold and silver coins. They would pay for the exotic cargoes of Oriental luxuries: the Chinese and Japanese silks and velvets, the spices, woven rugs, gems, pearls, ivory and elaborate jewelry and beautiful porcelain from China. There were also religious articles produced by the artisans of Asia, finely made of gold, silver, rare wood and ivory. These items, Antonio knew, would bring a handsome price, both at home and abroad.

Things went well at Macao. Antonio paid his way through much of the protocol and spent the better part of a year there, gradually loading his galleon with valuable merchandise. Several paying passengers signed on to make the return trip to Mexico when the ship was ready. Such travelers were not uncommon. Antonio had accommodated many such wayfarers in the past. Some returned to New Spain illegally.

The crew spent the last night on shore drinking and carousing into the early dawn and had to be hauled back to the ship in a stupor. After a few hours of sleep, they were refreshed, repaired, and ready for duty. The sobering process was accelerated when Antonio bellowed orders to "Prepare to sail!" Passengers were relegated to their section of the ship and cargoes were secured. The most difficult part lay ahead.

The return voyage usually took several months because the galleons had to travel the East China Sea as far north as Japan, at times, in order to catch the westerly winds necessary to transport them across the Pacific to the California coast. They would then proceed in a southerly direction to Acapulco. The trip was an arduous one and passengers and crew often fell victim to scurvy and other diseases or to exposure.

Antonio and Roberto stood at the helm with a good wind at their backs — the prayer of every sailor. The night was clear under a luminous and brightly-spangled sky. "We are lucky that the weather has held and the winds are favorable." Antonio looked at Roberto, who seemed to have something else on his mind.

"When we reach Acapulco and we clear with the authorities, we must make contact with certain friends in Mexico City. You follow my thoughts?" Roberto asked.

Their conversations were always guarded. The Inquisition had big ears. "I have planned for that," Antonio assured his friend. "When we complete our transactions, we will enjoy a visit with my Uncle Hector who lives in Acapulco. Then we shall decide about returning to Mexico City. Meanwhile, the ship will be secured and anchored in the harbor until arrangements have been made for the transfer of goods to other ports."

"What of our passengers? The ones who wish to go to Mexico City?" Roberto wondered.

"They will be met at the dock in Acapulco by friends, I am sure." He winked at Roberto, who understood. It meant that those who were New Christians would be met and welcomed by other New Christians and provided temporary shelter until they continued on their way to Mexico City, with their help. In most cases, these people were Secret Jews.

"That is good." Roberto was relieved. Now he turned his conversation in a more pleasant direction. "Meanwhile, we can enjoy our time at the Acapulco Fair which is regularly held when the galleons arrive, I hear. Is that not so?"

A huge grin creased Antonio's face as he nodded enthusiastically. "The fairs are always not only a good time but profitable. We shall unload many of the wares at the marketplace where they will bring a good price."

Merchants from miles around converged upon this strip of land to seek items from not only the Orient but also from India and the distant land of Persia. Acapulco lay between a fine harbor and surrounding mountains. Not an impressive town, it consisted of a dispersion of shacks, a small church and a fortress of less than admirable size. Only the arrival of the ships energized the sleepy little town. Now it was fiesta time!

What relief Antonio felt when he was cleared to disembark. He set his passengers ashore and then assigned his officers and crew to six-hour shifts, guarding and unloading the merchandise he specified. These alternating vigils allowed them shore leave for the satisfaction of their "thirsts."

Uncle Hector was ready and waiting. For several days, he sat gazing down from his window to the docks in the harbor. Finally, the galleons arrived and he knew his nephew would soon be knocking at his door. When Antonio and Roberto finally made their appearance, Uncle Hector was so happy, he flitted about them like a firefly. Antonio enveloped him in a bear hug — not a difficult thing to accomplish. Hector was a small man. Growing bald, his one remaining lock of hair was plastered across a high forehead.

"Uncle, how are you? Still losing your hair, I see, but your smile is as heartwarming as always," Antonio teased.

The uncle did not know how to handle this two-pronged comment but his face reflected his reaction — first, by drooping with embarrassment and then lighting up as a smile danced around his eyes. "Nephew, you are a malicious boy to tease me so."

"Come, come — you are my favorite uncle," Antonio cajoled.

"I am your only uncle. My sister, God rest her soul — her head would be revolving upon her shoulders if she knew what mischief you create." Hector dared not say more for he did not want to anger Antonio. What he had to tell him would be inflammatory enough. Thank the Lord, he had some good news to mollify the bad.

After sharing some wine and bread and cheese, Antonio demanded, "All right, Uncle. Have you heard any news from Mexico City? Is my family safe? When I left, the Holy Office was paying us a lot of attention. Damn it, I hope by now they have forgotten about me and the family."

"Nephew, the word I received is that they have knowledge of your voyage to the Orient. They had intended to impound your ship and its contents upon your return..."

"What?" Antonio rose to his feet, shouting. "Those miserable —" he fumed.

"Patience, nephew." Hector tried to assuage him, "Let me continue please. It is not as bad as it sounds. I heard they decided instead that you will pay a fine and turn over a percentage of your profits from the trip to the Inquisition. They are looking for a sum equal to what they consider to be your wife's worth."

"How did you learn of this, and how reliable is this information? How can I accomplish this? Oh, God, I must get back to my poor darlings. How is Catalina and my precious little daughter?" He grew increasingly emotional as he spoke.

Hector knew that if he did not stop Antonio, he would run the gamut from hysteria to rage. This Hector did not relish. His nephew could be one "*hombre malo*" when agitated. "A cousin of mine, in high places dispatched the information to me. He is someone to be trusted, believe me," Hector told him.

Roberto came to the rescue. "Antonio, this is the best thing that could have happened. When we return, you will provide the money they demand and they will drop the case against you. I am sure the money will change their perception of you." He sniggered. "Give them their pound of flesh 'in the name of the Lord Jesus Christ' and they will fall in love with you." The others joined him in a hearty laugh.

"We will beat them again, my friend. They will have to accept my accounting of our transactions, unless they want to launch a lengthy investigation. The greedy ones will not do that for they want the money, pronto. I shall be generous, but they will never be able to estimate the true extent of our dealings. Meanwhile, my dear ones, they will have to find me first!" When he uttered these last words, Antonio's well-defined features hardened and contorted into a sneer. "Let the dogs eat dirt!"

Uncle Hector quaked.

CHAPTER XIV

THE RETURN

A lone figure in friar's cloak and hood walked slowly toward the Great Square in Mexico City. It was late in the day and people were hurrying to their homes for the dinner hour. The chimes of the cathedral rang out for vespers. Those who noticed the friar made quick little signs of deference to which he responded in kind. Proceeding to the farthest corner of the Square, the fray turned down Calle Cinqo to Avenida de la Fe. His pace quickened and soon he arrived at one particular house. Before knocking at the door, he stood awhile, meticulously observing any activity on the street.

When Catalina opened the front door, her automatic reaction was that the fray was collecting alms for the needy. It was not unusual for these frocked servants of the Church to go from house to house. Catalina mused, *Why do they not show themselves? Always the covered head and the long, cumbersome robe.* "Please, come in, fray, and sit down for a few minutes. I shall get a donation for you."

Nodding, he sat in the nearest chair. When Catalina returned and handed him five pesos, she was amazed at his response. "It will take more than five pesos to satisfy me, Senora." The hoarse voice frightened her. She stammered, "But...but...padre...if you find this inadequate, I shall be only too happy to give more..."

"You will give me all you possess, my darling Catalina." He threw back his hood, swooped her up in his arms and whirled her about, all the while laughing uproariously.

Shock and amazement were immediately transformed into happy recognition. "My God, Antonio! What...? Where...?" She could barely put words together.

"Come, my sweet — let us have some wine to celebrate our reunion. But, first, where is my beloved daughter, my Leonor? How she must have grown since I left — and you, my precious wife, how you must have suffered!"

"Leonor is with her grandmother. They went for their evening walk and should be back shortly."

Both had tears in their eyes as Antonio embraced the wife he had not seen in over two years. He whispered endearingly as he held her tightly to him, inhaling the fragrance of her, kissing the softness of her long tresses and feeling the familiar curves of her body.

"My husband, let us go to the table. We can talk while we enjoy some wine and the supper I have prepared. You must be hungry."

"Hungry? Yes, for you, my love. Antonio scooped her up in his arms and carried the giggling Catalina up the stairs to their bedroom.

Little Leonor held Grandma Francisca's hand as she skipped along the path to the house. They had taken their usual early evening promenade around the Square. It was not only for exercise and fresh air that Francisca did this. She kept her eyes and ears open for any information she could glean regarding the Inquisition's activities. It was amazing what could be learned from conversations on the street.

Opening the front door, she was puzzled by the scene that confronted her. The table was set as usual, but on the floor nearby was an overturned chair and what looked like a long, brown cape — a friar's cloak. Catalina was nowhere in sight. A sudden fear gripped Francisca. Could a commissary of the Inquisition have arrested Catalina? My God, Catalina and her sister Leonor had just had their "penances" lifted and had shed their sanbenitos. As the poor woman stood there agonizing over the unknown, suddenly the sound of laughter mingled with moans and exclamations came filtering down from upstairs. A smile played around her lips. Memory served her well. Such sounds could mean only one thing. Her granddaughter tugged at her skirt and demanded, "Why is Mama making little screams? Is someone hurting her?"

"Not at all, little one," Francisca answered, amused. "Quite the contrary. I think your Mama is a most happy lady right now." To herself, she muttered, "So, that rascal of a son-in-law is back." She sighed. "Bueno."

When the little girl saw her father coming down the stairs, she squealed with delight and ran into his outstretched arms. "Papa, Papa, where have you been? I looked for you every day. I am so happy to see you, my dear papa."

Antonio lifted her high into the air and her shrieks of pleasure evoked both smiles and tears, as the two women watched. For a brief moment, they were a carefree, happy family enjoying a reunion. Francisca served the meal and, as they enjoyed the repast, Antonio told them all that had transpired since his hasty departure. Then it was Catalina's turn to bring him up-to-date on the family's situation.

Luis' sister Mariana, released from hospital, came to live with Antonio and Catalina. She was a lovely girl, still single because of a romance that had ended abruptly a few years ago, through no fault of hers. The villain then had been Antonio who, in one of his erratic moods, had announced that he would take Mariana as wife #2, regardless of his being married to Catalina. After many stormy arguments, Francisca had finally impressed upon him that having more than one wife was frowned upon and no longer acceptable. "Who do you think you are," she demanded, "one of the old Jews in the Bible?"

Antonio, furious at first, calmed down and agreed to abandon his idea. Unfortunately, during the course of the controversy, the young man whom Mariana truly loved decided that discretion was the better part of valor and removed himself to parts unknown. Poor Mariana suffered terribly and was devastated by the loss of her love.

As the months passed, she had become morbid and irrational at times. Eventually the stress had such a debilitating affect upon her behavior that she would often endure manic depressive cycles. The family lived in fear of those cycles. It was especially frightening when there were visitors in the house. During her bouts of erratic behavior, Mariana had often babbled nonsensically and spewed irreligious profanities in front of visiting clergy and nuns. Luckily, they had considered her "a poor, sick girl who does not know what she is saying." On one occasion, she suddenly appeared nude, declaring, "I am the Holy Mother and you must hold me in reverence." There had been a lot of hurrying and scurrying to get her out of the room. The visiting priest had attributed her strange actions to her illness, aware that she had been hospitalized in the past.

After Mariana lived with Catalina and Antonio for awhile, her actions became intolerable again. Antonio reached a point where he became abusive. More and more, he regarded her as a threat. She spoke blasphemies in front of the wrong audience. He constantly berated her. "You crazy girl. You will be the death of us."

Francisca and Catalina suggested institutionalizing Mariana again. Antonio would not hear of it. "We cannot chance it. What if she speaks of the clandestine activities in the house — of the prayer meetings and observance of Jewish rituals? You are crazier than she is to even think of it."

"You make a good point," Francisca agreed, "but, nevertheless, we must get some professional help so that we may know how to care for her. In that way, we shall control the situation."

"No!" shouted Antonio. "Nobody comes to this house to observe her." With that, he stormed out, slamming the door hard.

The women thought that perhaps he gone to seek advice from someone he can trust. They were hopeful. When he returned, however, he stormed back into the house and Catalina could tell that he had been drinking. The smell of liquor trailed Antonio as he passed them on his way up the stairs to Mariana's room. Within minutes, cries of torment emanated from the chamber. Mother and daughter almost fell over each other as they hastened up the stairs. Before they got to it, the door was flung open and an inebriated, surly Antonio greeted them with, "See, I shall soon have this problem solved."

As they looked past the lurching figure at the screaming Mariana, Francisca yelled in a horrified voice, "You fool, what have you done to her?" She rushed to Mariana's bed where the girl had been trussed up like a captured animal. "You beast," Francisca screamed. "We shall speak to Luis about this."

That comment had a sobering influence on Antonio. He did not relish a confrontation with his brother-in-law, so he proceeded to assuage the women. "Come now," he coaxed, "I meant no harm. I thought it might bring her around if I displayed some firmness. You know, like disciplining a naughty child. I promise you, I shall not upset her again."

Francisca warned, "If you so much as touch her again, you will pay dearly — I guarantee it."

Several days later, an incident occurred which could have proven of great detriment to the de Carvajals. Mariana, in a pique, picked up several religious statues from the Catholic chapel in the house and hurled them about, muttering obscenities. In a state of panic, her sister and brother-in-law rushed around trying to pick up the pieces and to quiet Mariana's shouts. Before they could grab her, she had tossed one of the figurines out of the window. Antonio dashed from the house to retrieve it. A neighbor stood nearby and watched with curiosity. The loud voices had attracted him, but he understood not a word. Antonio hastily picked up the shards, explaining hurriedly, "I was standing by the window to get more light while I was admiring this statuette and — I do not know how it happened — somehow it slipped from my hand." With a nervous laugh, he turned away and rushed back into the house, bolting the door behind him.

Catalina was applying wet compresses to Mariana's head. The girl was sobbing uncontrollably as Francisca patted her hands in an attempt to calm her down.

Antonio said, "Thanks to God, nothing bad will come of this. I explained to our neighbor that it was a slip of the hand. I am sure he believed me." He placed an arm around Mariana. "Be calm, little sister. All is well." To his wife, he suggested, "Let us recite a prayer for our safety."

A few days later, Justa and Luis came to visit. While they were chatting and enjoying the meal, Mariana suddenly made an announcement that disrupted the pleasant afternoon. "I shall go voluntarily to the Inquisition and martyr myself." If a bomb had been dropped in their midst, it would have been less devastating.

"My dear," Luis jumped to her side, "do not entertain such thoughts. It will mean death not only for you, but also for your loved ones."

Mariana started to raise her voice. "I will take what I see is the proper action. I must tell the 'evil ones' what the truth is. I must free them from their 'blindness' and I am willing to die to do this."

"No, no, my sweet sister. It is not God's will that you sacrifice yourself. There is much work to be done here with your people and I need your help." Luis held her in his arms and gently stroked her hair.

"Are you sure, Luis?" she whimpered. "Is it God's will that I do His work here?"

"Yes, my darling. We all love you and need you."

"Yes, for sure," added Justa.

"All right, my loved ones. I shall go to bed now. I am exhausted." She looked like a tired child who had played too hard for too long. Luis kissed her lightly on the forehead and Francisca led her away.

All uttered a sigh of relief.

CHAPTER XV

PENANCE AND PERIL

The years 1591 to early 1594 were the best years for the family, even though the ever-present fear of the Inquisition was as much a part of their daily lives as was breathing. With the exception of the absence of Jorge and her sons, Miguel and Baltasar, Francisca managed to fair relatively well with her other siblings.

In 1591, Leonor's sentence had ended, as did Catalina's; Mariana's ended in 1592. Outwardly, the "penitent ones" religiously pursued and maintained the vestiges of the Catholic faith they had sworn "to live and die by" when the Inquisition had sentenced them. In order to avoid the stake, many had followed the path of conversion. Of course, this did not mean, for one moment, that they had forsaken God, the Lord of Israel. They worshipped in the Catholic faith publicly; secretly they said their prayers to Adonai, always asking for forgiveness and salvation. "Almighty God, may the prayers of the lost fill your heart with mercy and forgiveness, knowing we are not truly lost but ever devoted to your glorification," they intoned.

As the days progressed, the family enjoyed a fairly peaceful, ordinary life in spite of the demanding conditions under which they existed. Little Ánica had been returned to the family after a stay of two years with the Catholic family to whom she had been sent during the trial. While there, unfortunately, she suffered from a throat ailment, the improper diagnosis of which resulted in a medical procedure that caused irreparable harm to her vocal chords. The child had difficulty in expressing herself and only her sister Leonor understood her best.

Mariana's condition improved gradually and she took a personal and caring interest in helping her little sister. Francisca and the girls set about diligently to reorient Anica into their Jewish practices. Anica applied herself willingly.

Apparently having resolved the "demons" within herself, Mariana now attended the School for Girls. She was contented and shared her free time with her siblings. Her behavior was exemplary. As her mother would say, "It is another miracle, blessed be His name."

Luis spent most of his time traveling to the outlying districts of Mexico City. There he had not only friends with whom he met and prayed regularly, but also the monasteries wherein he presented his letters of recommendation in pursuit of eliciting the "ransom" demanded for the family's freedom; he was often invited to remain as a guest. These credentials provided him with access to people and places where he was well received. It amazed Luis how willing and cooperative they were. In addition to money, contributors often bestowed upon him foodstuffs, such as cheese, vegetables and poultry — items he was able to bring home to his mother's house, which was still the designated place of their imprisonment.

When he stayed at the monasteries, his biggest problem was the preparation of the food offered him. On most occasions, he declined their hospitality, using a variety of excuses, always careful not to arouse the suspicion that his rejection stemmed from the fact that the food was not prepared according to Jewish dietary laws.

On one of Luis' visits home, Francisca carefully observed her son. He looked so gaunt, she thought. After serving him a generous helping of his favorite dish — *arroz con pollo* — she remarked, "You are so thin, my son. Are you eating properly?"

"Mother, that is a problem for me when I am on the road. How can I eat food prepared with lard, or the pork that is served at the monasteries? Unfortunately, it is to these places that I must go, for the most part, to seek alms. One of the excuses I offer is to say that I have already eaten. Often I only have some bread which I manage to salvage and I do not have even that until I am alone in the woods, where I can eat and pray under God's canopy, under the stars."

As always, Francisca was enraptured by Luis' way of expressing himself. "Oh, Luis, you are indeed a poet. 'God's canopy.' How beautiful! But you cannot live on bread alone."

"I promise you, Mother, that I shall try to eat more." He nudged her playfully and they both laughed. Hollow words, he thought, but for the moment they served their purpose. He continued. "What I am truly concerned about is that raising the money to buy our freedom takes precious time away from my activities as a teacher and proselytizer. But I must not deliberate over this. The ransom will buy our rehabilitation and that is what is essential at the moment. Yes, this is my priority. Soon we shall be free and I shall take my place among our people, to enlighten them and sing the praises of the God of Israel, blessed be His name."

"Yet," Francisca agonized, "I worry so when you are away. There is so much danger! How can you know whom to trust?"

Luis comforted her. "Do not fret, Mother. Think of your son as one of the pilgrims of the Lord. It is God's will that I gather charity to save us. It is His intercession that permits me to do so. And as I follow this path and spread the word of the Law of Moses, many are returning to the Old Religion."

Still, Francisca's fears were not allayed and she persisted. "I fear for you; I know you are careful but we are surrounded by enemies. Even a hint to the Inquisition — oh, I cannot bear the thought." She wept.

An anguished Luis looked at this beautiful human being who had suffered so terribly at the hands of her torturers — how hard she had tried to be brave. Surely she is on God's list of those who will be rewarded in Heaven. Hugging her, he said lovingly, "Please, Mother dear, I promise you — all will be well. Soon we shall have our freedom, and I shall take you and all my dear ones to another country where we shall worship openly and without fear."

In a bare whisper, Francisca said, "From your mouth to God's ears, my precious one."

On one of his trips, while visiting his friend Manuel de Lucena in Pachuca, Luis learned that another friend, Pedro Navarro, was ill. "Let us visit him and pray together for his recovery, Manuel. I shall bring Justa with me. She is like medicine. Her lively personality will cheer him up."

Manuel agreed. "And I shall bring my wife. It will be a reunion for us. Circumstances hardly permit us to spend time together anymore."

"I know," Luis answered. "I am so involved in raising the money for our releases, I barely have a moment to spare."

On his way back to his mother's house, Luis stopped by briefly to invite Justa. He kissed her quickly on the cheek and advised her to be ready at noon the next day. "Until tomorrow, my love." He then hastened to see his loved ones for a brief overnight visit.

The next morning, after a late breakfast, he bade them goodbye and left for Justa's house. When he arrived there, she rushed to the door to greet him with the gleeful emotion and youthful exuberance typical of an uninhibited girl in love. "Luis, I missed you so! I am glad you have asked me to accompany you to see Pedro and I shall see Manuel and Teresa again, too. I am so happy!" Then remembering the reason for their visit, she said apologetically, "I am sorry Pedro is so ill. It is sinful for me to feel joy at this moment. Forgive me, Luis, but I do love you so much that it is difficult for me to repress my feelings."

He kissed her ardently and held her in a crushing embrace. Her sweet face reflected the passion within her. She looked like a little girl who had just had her most fervent wish fulfilled. In effect, it was not far from the truth.

Luis urged, "Come, my sweet — we must leave now if we are to arrive before dark. The roads can be treacherous at night."

Her mother watched as Justa settled into her seat behind Luis on his horse, wrapping her arms around his waist and pressing her cheek against his back. "God be with you, children," Clara called after them. Within moments, they were gone from view.

Upon their arrival, they found their friends engaged in prayer. The pair waited respectfully until the completion of the recitation and then greeted each other warmly. Pedro was in a somewhat improved condition. Manuel and Teresa had maintained a vigil for almost a week, looking to his every need. He was influenced by Manuel whom he respected but he revered Luis, whose reputation as a leader of Secret Jews was impressive.

They enjoyed a repast before engaging in a theological discussion. Pedro could hardly wait. With Luis here, it was truly an occasion. As they sat talking, Domingo, Pedro's older brother, entered the room. With a flicker of his eyelids, Pedro sent a message that the conversation should change its course. Manuel and Luis followed his lead even though the cryptic warning puzzled them. For most of the evening, they engaged in light conversation.

Gradually, Manuel's curiosity got the best of him and several times he tried to steer the discussion towards religious dogma. He wondered if Domingo was a Secret Jew. Very often, within the same family, there was a difference of religious adherence. As Manuel pressed on, Pedro kept clearing his throat and rolling his eyes but his friend was undaunted. He had to know.

After listening to Manuel's preachings for an hour or so, Domingo finally lashed out at him for "trying to convert a good Christian." So saying, he took his leave.

Luis had said nothing the entire time. Poor, sick Pedro was frantic. "I apologize for my brother but, Manuel, you would not heed my signals. Domingo is a dedicated Catholic. I am always careful to avoid conversations of a religious nature with him. He may be my brother but I do not trust him. I fear him."

Manuel and Luis attempted to make light of the situation, but the glances they exchanged betrayed their innermost feelings.

114

When Luis and Justa returned to Mexico City, they stopped to see Catalina and Antonio. Anxious to know if Antonio had settled his "account" with the Inquisition, Luis inquired, "Antonio, are you in the good graces of the Holy Office yet? It will not be long before our redemption papers arrive and I have almost the entire 850 pesos to pay for them. A few more trips and it is done."

"Do not worry about me," Antonio assured him. "I have donated my pound of flesh. They practically kissed me, the mercenary devils."

Catalina could not help laughing at her husband's comments.

"I am glad it is settled. We must be careful to avoid any suspicion or to create any antagonism," Luis suggested. "When we buy our freedom, I shall make arrangements for all of us to leave this wretched place. Get your house in order, my dear ones." He winked at them knowingly. Everyone knew what that advice meant: consolidate holdings and assets for quick liquidation in case a hasty departure became necessary.

Luis changed the subject. "Where is my darling niece, Leonor? I want to give her a big hug and kiss before I leave for our mother's house." He looked around questioningly.

His sister answered, cheerfully, "I will bring her to you. She is upstairs, napping."

"No, no." Luis placed a restraining hand on Catalina's arm. "I will go quietly to her bedside. Do not wake her." He tiptoed into the child's bedroom and approached the sleeping figure. *How beautiful and angelic she is*, he thought. As he bent to kiss her lightly on the cheek, Leonor suddenly opened her eyes. When she recognized her uncle, she cried out with happiness, stretching her little arms eagerly towards him.

"Uncle Luis, where have you been? I missed you so. Can we go horseback riding?"

He laughed at her impetuosity. "Yes, yes, little one, but not now. Go back to your siesta. I will come for you tomorrow morning and we shall go for a ride. Today, my horse is very, very tired and I must take him home so he may rest. All right?"

"Yes, Uncle. I shall wait for you after breakfast." She hugged him, then pursing her lips, she kissed him loudly on the cheek.

Hesitating for a brief moment, he looked at this sweet, innocent child and prayed that he will be able to rescue her and the whole family from this madness. He was grateful that she was too young to fully comprehend the perils they faced. "God grant us exodus from this horror so that she may grow up in a free land."

CHAPTER XVI

CLOSE ENCOUNTERS

A young man in a sanbenito, bearing the cross of St. Andrew on it, and a young lady simply, but tastefully dressed, entered the Cathedral in the Great Square. They walked down the central aisle to the altar, genuflected, then made their way to the tiers of candles at the side. Each lifted a taper, lighted it from the flames of candles already burning and carefully set two more aflame. They extinguished the tapers in a pot of sand, knelt before their offerings with heads lowered, and silently recited a prayer. After a few moments, the pair rose, genuflected once more at the altar, and hastened to the exit in the rear.

Outside in the bright sunlight, they took a deep breath. Justa linked her arm with Luis' as he smiled warmly at her. "Well done, my darling. I am sure anyone observing us was properly impressed by our act of devotion. We must leave no doubt as to where our loyalties lie."

"I know, beloved, you are concerned about the incident at Pedro's house but Domingo is his brother. Surely he would do him no harm." Justa tried to assuage Luis' fears. "I am sure it was just a little family disagreement, nothing more."

"Darling, you are probably right. But somehow I am apprehensive about that man. It is obvious Domingo has totally divorced himself from his true heritage. Many "*conversos*" often become fanatic about their conversion and, at times, are more of a threat than the Old Christians. Let us hope that he is not."

As they spoke, they walked past the Holy Office headquarters and Casa Chata, the jail to which the family had originally been taken. Luis shivered as memories returned. Justa saw him quicken his pace and she fell into step alongside him. She suggested, "My love, let us buy some flowers from that vendor in the Square. You know how much your mother loves them. We shall bring her a bouquet."

"Good idea, Justa. Flowers always make her smile."

With blossoms in one hand and his other arm around Justa's waist, Luis led her across the plaza, then down the Street of the Old Canal where his mother resided with his sisters. The old stone adobes, remnants of a time long gone, lined a street that had once bordered on a lovely canal. However, since the invasion of the early conquistadors, the clean, fresh waterways that were so cherished by the ancients became nothing more than landfills of garbage and dirt. As they approached the house, Fray Pedro suddenly appeared in the open doorway. He immediately embraced Luis, saying, "I was just visiting your family. Dear boy, it is good to see you again. We all miss you at the Colegia. I hear that you have been successful in collecting the alms for your release. The Lord has blessed you and soon you will be redeemed. You and the family will take your place in our society as good Christians. The unfortunate events of the past shall be erased."

"Yes, Padre, so they shall," Luis answered with sincerity. "I cannot express how grateful I am for your help and cooperation." Luis loved the old friar.

Fray Pedro blessed him, made the sign of the cross and bade them goodnight.

Inside the house, Francisca could hardly wait to embrace her son. As soon as the fray left, she welcomed them and within minutes was in the kitchen preparing an array of homemade delicacies. Soon the table was abundant with some of Luis' favorite dishes. He flashed a mischievous smile at Justa as he teased his mother about her fetish for feeding him every time she set eyes upon him.

"This is why I do not come home more often," he jested. "You want to fatten me up *como un puerco* for slaughter." He laughed as she complained about his comparison to a pig but he wrapped his arms around her and danced her about the room.

A persistent knock at the door interrupted the giddy scene. Isabel and Leonor, who were just entering the room, froze in their tracks, motionless as stone. The knocking continued, accompanied now by a loud voice demanding that someone come to the door.

Francisca called, "Un momento, por favor!" She looked at Luis questioningly. He signaled her to open the door after they all assumed a relaxed pose at the dining room table.

"Senora de Carvajal?" Two men stood in the entranceway. Luis recognized one as a commissary of the Inquisition.

"Si, I am she. What do you wish?" she asked, with as much control as she could muster.

One of the men handed her a document bearing the seal of the Holy Office. It was a summons for her and her children to appear before General Inquisitor Peralta the next morning to answer some questions. Just seeing that name sent waves of terror through Luis. How vividly he recalled the brutality they had endured because of him. *What was happening,* he wondered. *Everything had seemed to be going so well.*

Every one of them knew the horrendous fate that would be in store if charges of 'relapsing' were brought against them. Luis tried to console his mother and siblings. "Do not fear, dear ones — it is probably an audience to determine if we have raised the money to pay for our freedom."

"Oh, my son, do you really think so? Or has someone betrayed us?" She began to cry. Within minutes, his sisters joined in the wailing. It broke his heart to see them all so terrified.

"Please, please, my darlings. You have nothing to fear. Almighty God, blessed be His name, shall deliver us from the enemy as He has done so many times before."

Another sleepless night.

In the morning, before they left for the Hall of the Inquisition, Luis led them in a recitation of the Shema Israel, the prayer that acknowledges One Universal God. Then they quietly filed out into the nearly deserted street where some early risers were hurrying to early mass at the Cathedral. It was just before twilight; the sky was still laden with deep shadows, but here and there a sliver of light fractured the darkness. The de Carvajals walked in silence, each struggling with his or her innermost sinister thoughts.

The fleshy-faced custodian at the Inquisition Hall looked up from his desk when they presented themselves. Although impassive, he was not unfriendly. He remarked, "De Carvajal...hmm, yes, I remember you from Casa Chata a few years ago."

Luis peered at him. "Ah, yes." This was the guard who had been helpful — for a price — on several occasions during their incarceration. This might prove helpful.

Lowering his voice, the custodian asked, "Is there a problem again?"

"We do not know why we are here," Luis replied, and softly added, "but, if for some reason, we are detained..." Luis put his hand in his pocket where he had several ducats and a slip of paper upon which he had written Antonio de Caceres' name and address. He had prepared for just such an exigency — with God's help. Luis slipped the money and note into the guard's hand and whispered instructions.

"It is done, Senor," the guard assured him, quickly hiding the items in his vest. He remembered how lucrative his previous favors had proven.

The family stood before Alonso de Peralta, summoning up as much courage as they could, under the circumstances. Luis looked at the inquisitor's face — the same menacing veneer, the strong features over strong bones, complemented by ferret-like eyes that were cold and piercing. He said nothing for several minutes, obviously relishing how disconcerting this was to his visitors. Suddenly, as if someone had flipped a switch, Peralta grew animated. His eyes focused on them with an almost benign expression as he made them welcome. "Well, well, I am happy to see the de Carvajals again, only under different circumstances this time." He chuckled.

The ambiguity puzzled them and yet offered a ray of hope. They listened carefully as he continued. "The Holy Office has scheduled an auto-da-fe in November at which time those found guilty of heresy and not reconciled with the Church shall go to the fire."

Luis' mind was racing. What was he driving at? He wished he would get on with it. Aloud, he protested, "Sir, we have been faithful in our devotion to Jesus Christ ever since our sentencing and have performed our penances without omission —"

The outburst astonished Peralta, yet from past experience, he would not have expected less from this young man. He recalled what a strong adversary he had been during his interrogations. "Luis, you misunderstand," the inquisitor continued. "I have no quarrel with you or your family here in Mexico City. Fray Pedro has often reported the exemplary behavior of the de Carvajals."

Taking the offensive, Luis asked, "What is it that you wish of us?" Whatever they had to face, they would face it with strength and dignity. Studying Peralta's face, he thought, *Bastardo*, to put us through this torture. He looked at his mother and sisters with an encouraging expression. Poor things, they look so distraught. His expression changed when he turned to Peralta, who was now speaking.

"We are concerned with your brothers Baltasar and Miguel; also, your brother-in-law, Jorge de Almeida. They were never apprehended and reconciled with the Church. Indeed, it is a known fact that they have escaped to safe haven in Europe. We intend to convict them in absentia and then burn them in effigy on All Saints' Day, November 1st, at the auto-da-fe."

The women gasped. Burning even images was a disconcerting, unbearable thought. They exchanged glances with Luis, still at a loss as to why they were there being told of the Holy Office's plans. Peralta's next statement answered their questions. "You have been called in to give testimony as to the Judaizing of Jorge, Baltasar, and Miguel. Your sworn statements are essential for the record. Do you have any objections to cooperating in this matter?"

Relief flooded Luis' being. Now he knew the course he must take. He understood full well what the Holy Office was really after. It was nothing new. They wanted to requisition any money and property still remaining in New Spain that belonged to Jorge and Baltasar; Miguel was too young to have accumulated any real property. Luis himself had made all the arrangements for the transfer of such holdings and had sent whatever funds he could salvage to Jorge via friends traveling abroad. The men were safe; the Inquisition could not touch them. "What is it you wish us to do?" Luis asked and glanced at his loved ones, knowing they would follow his lead.

"Do you agree to give testimony to the fact that these men were Judaizers while they lived in Mexico City, that they pretended to be conversos, that they did not reconcile with the Church before they escaped?" Peralta asked.

It took but a moment for Luis to agree and the others to follow suit. After all, this could do the men no harm, and cooperating with Peralta would enhance their position. The Holy Office shall have its Pyrrhic victory.

Obviously anticipating their consent, a prepared document was presented to them that they each signed. A commissary, who had taken notes of the proceedings, asked for a sworn affirmation as well. Next to where he sat on a platform was a huge cross. He told them, "Each of you will approach the cross, one at a time, kiss it and answer 'Yes' to the question, 'Were Jorge de Almeida, Baltasar de Carvajal, and Miguel de Carvajal converts who, in fact, were secretly practicing the Law of Moses?"

Francisca went first, then the girls. Luis was the last and after he answered, he added, "They are Jews and devoted to the God of the Law of Moses." His demeanor disguised the pride with which he uttered these words and the satisfaction it gave him.

This added incrimination elated Peralta who missed the subtle inflection in Luis' voice. He welcomed the indisputable corroboration of guilt.

"Magnus Dominus et laudabilis nimis." Great is the Lord and highly to be praised.

The thought passed through the minds of both men, but for different reasons.

CHAPTER XVII

DIRE STRAITS

Domingo Navarro scurried across the Great Square, his glances darting from one side to the other. He hoped that no one would notice him as he went to the side entrance of the Cathedral. Once inside, he hastened to the nearest empty confessional. *My conscience has plagued me long enough*, he thought. *It is time to relieve myself of my guilt*. He stepped into the booth. The sound of the door latch snapping into place strengthened his resolve.

With his knees on the worn, velvet pillow on the floor, he waited for a few minutes. Then through the aperture, he barely discerned the familiar frocked figure of a priest taking his seat on the other side of the wall that separated them.

Domingo began, "Forgive me, Father, for I have sinned."

"My son, how have you sinned?" the priest asked.

Recognizing the voice of Father Benardo, Domingo felt more at ease. "I have kept a secret for a long time. But I can no longer bear the burden — the heartache and the pain. I must tell you all."

"Go on, my boy," the priest encouraged him.

"I have suspected for some time that my brother Pedro is a Secret Jew and that only for appearances does he live his life as a New Christian."

"Are you certain of this, my son? What proof do you have? I am sure you are aware of what action can result from such charges."

"Certainly," Domingo answered, "but as a true Christian I am compelled to report the truth — even if it is my own brother. Is that not so, Father?"

"Yes. Please, go on. Tell me what you know," he persisted.

Domingo narrated the events of the visit to his sick brother Pedro — how he had observed Manuel de Lucena and his wife discussing the Law of Moses, how Lucena had tried to involve him in the conversation — no doubt in an attempt to convert him "I vehemently rejected all of their blasphemies, Father," Domingo assured his mentor.

"Admirable. What you must do now is report this to the Holy Office. You have tormented yourself long enough." The cleric made the sign of the cross. "May the Lord Jesus Christ guide you and protect you" and so saying, he quickly and silently vanished.

Domingo continued to kneel. Having verbalized what had tormented him for so long, he felt a tremendous sense of relief. Before he could take that irreversible step to the chambers of the Inquisition, he had needed consolation and affirmation through confession. Now his determination and a sense of deep, religious conviction paved the path across the plaza to the Holy Office. There he requested an immediate audience on an "extremely urgent matter to the Inquisition."

A clerk ushered him into a large, sparsely furnished sitting room and told him to wait. Settling into one of the only two available chairs, the penitent one squirmed nervously on the hard, wooden seat. Finally, the door opened and an imposing figure in a long, black robe entered. He took his place across from Domingo and in a voice that would frighten any contrite heart, demanded, "Why have you requested an audience?" Alonso de Peralta held a folder through which he continued to scan as he addressed Domingo. "Identify yourself."

"Sir, I am Domingo Navarro, brother of Pedro Navarro, about whom I have come to the Holy Office." He proceeded to repeat the details of his confession to Father Benardo. Peralta made some notations, then stopped Domingo from continuing. "I shall send for a scribe to record your story, so it may be entered accurately in the report I shall make."

When the secretary arrived, Peralta advised Domingo to recount the facts he had given thus far. "Senor Navarro," Peralta resumed, "who else was present during that visit to your brother's house?"

"Luis de Carvajal and Justa Mendez, but they did not contribute or participate in any manner."

Peralta's eyes narrowed. The mention of Luis de Carvajal's name came as a shock. Early that same morning, Luis, his mother, and his oldest sister, Isabel, had appeared before the Inquisitional Court. The 850 pesos required for their liberty had been paid and their sanbenitos removed. The official releases had arrived from Spain with the first fleet in September. All the reports about the family's behavior were flawless. Now this?

Peralta leaned forward and patted Domingo's hand. "You have acted as a good Christian. Your information is important. After all, we must ferret out these Judaizers and make examples of them. The reconciled who swear to follow the Evangelical Law and then revert to their evil, secret practices must be punished." Peralta's voice grew more forceful and 'hell and damnation' reverberated in every phrase.

Domingo sat as though turned to stone. Dread filled him. He prayed, *May I never stand accused of any misdeed before this judge. He is terrifying!*

Regaining his composure, the inquisitor made a most magnanimous gesture. He invited his trembling visitor to take coffee with him.

That same evening, the de Carvajals and friends were gathered in the prayer room of Francisca's house. They were celebrating the events of that morning — their deliverance from their sentences. Gone were the sanbenitos. They had watched as the tunics were be hung on the walls of the Cathedral, to be a reminder forever, and gone was the mandatory housing. They had secured their releases with an admonition from Dr. Lobo Guerrero to "live as good Christians."

Now, at home, they expressed their happiness in prayers and song. As Luis recited selections from his work, Justa admired his talent and thought, *He is a born leader, so learned. And he was her soul mate*, she vowed. When Luis concluded his last song, he addressed the congregation. "You are my flock. I humble myself before the Lord, unworthy, for He has chosen me to be the shepherd of His people who shall someday dwell in the land of Israel. I stand ready to defend His word with my life."

A pounding on the front door attended these words. Everyone quickly went downstairs to the living room. Francisca moved hesitantly toward the door, calling, *"Un momento,* I am coming." Opening the door, warily, she sighed with relief. "Ah, it is you, Arturo. Come in, welcome."

"I rushed here as quickly as I could," he blurted out. "Have you heard about the arrests?"

Arrests! The word conveyed instant terror. Worried glances were exchanged. Luis took command. "What are you telling us, *primo*? Who?"

"It is your friend Manuel, his wife, and also Pedro Navarro..." He was wringing his hands and his eyes were wet and red-rimmed. "I have just come from Casa Chata where I learned the news. That rotten Domingo — it was he who went to the Inquisition this morning. He made enough threats to his poor brother and now —" Arturo broke down.

At first inaudible, the voices in the room rose and mingled with mournful expressions of shock and fear. A hoarse-voiced Luis made an impassioned plea. "My dear ones, please stop the hysteria. We must get the details and discuss this quietly and sensibly." *How does one do this*, he wondered. He turned to Arturo, "Tell us everything you know."

The diminutive figure looked haggard. He blew his nose again and again, interjecting details between sniffles. "Early this morning, the Inquisition sent commissaries to the homes of the Lucenas and Pedro Navarro. They were taken into custody and brought to Casa Chata for interrogation..." He began to sob. "My God, we shall all die!"

Luis tried to allay his panic. Every one was reacting. "Cousin, please calm yourself. The matter will be resolved. Domingo cannot prove anything. It is his word against theirs." Luis wondered if that dog mentioned seeing him and Justa? How long would it be before...He did not finish the thought.

A disconsolate Arturo continued. "I stopped by the jail again to see if our rotund little friend was on duty. He has been helpful in the past. Indeed, there he was and a few ducats loosened his tongue." Arturo's face took on an expression of unspeakable pain. "He told me that the three victims were taken to the lower cells where they await a verdict. Meanwhile, he fears that they will be subjected to torture until they are forced to confess to the charges of Judaizing." He wiped his eyes again and continued, "I shall go to the jail again tomorrow and report back with any news."

The prayer group dispersed, a few at a time, and Justa bade the family goodnight. Her lashes were wet with unshed tears as she quickly kissed Luis on the cheek when he escorted her to the door. Clara, leaving with her daughter, said a solemn "May we meet again on a good day."

Left alone, the family sat around the kitchen table and attempted to decipher the implications of this latest development. A restive, nervous Isabel, exclaimed, "What could have prompted Domingo to turn in his own brother and his friends? The man must be a misguided fanatic...His own brother! It is not as though he was under threat of death or even incarceration."

"Imagine — he went to the Holy Office of his own free will." Francisca shook her head in disbelief.

Luis sat meditating. *Why have they not come for me?* He was to ask that question many times during the next months. At this particular moment, however, he attributed his freedom to God's miraculous intervention. Saved, like Joseph in Egypt. He sensed God's presence with him and he was at peace.

It was September 1594, and that meant it would soon be time to observe the Great Day (Yom Kippur) which is the last day of the Jewish New Year. The plan was for the family to spend the eve and the day of observance with Antonio and Catalina at their home. The celebration of this day is a solemn one and its observance demands the strictest adherence: fasting, long hours of prayer, self-searching, and confessions of sins. It is the day when God is asked to listen to the entreaties of forgiveness and to grant absolution.

The de Carvajals invited Justa and Clara to join them, as well as other friends and relatives. Enough food had been prepared and set aside for the 'breaking of the fast' as well, after sundown of the Great Day. When the last rays of light diffused with the oncoming darkness of evening, with fasting and praying concluded, all gathered around the table, replete with healthy appetites, to enjoy the traditional "breaking of the fast."

"Now, my loved ones, let us hope that we are forgiven our sins and trespasses and that the slates have been wiped clean." Luis lifted his glass of wine. "We start anew. May the good Lord bless us and protect us. To life!"

"To life!" their voices added, in unison.

After fruit compote, Justa passed around a tray of her popular apple fritters. She loved baking this delicacy because it was one of Luis' favorites. Francisca served cups of Turkish coffee. Momentarily forgotten was the anguish of recent events. She looked around at her loved ones gathered there and tears of happiness welled up in her eyes. Joy abounded in the house that holiday.

When they finished their dessert, Justa pleaded, "Luis, please, let us go for a walk. It is such a lovely night."

Luis did not wish to be rude, but his mother encouraged the idea. She loved Justa and had hopes that she and Luis would marry someday. "Go, children, go. The girls will help me straighten up. When you return, Luis will sing a hymn or two for us. Yes?"

"Of course, Mother." Luis knew how much she enjoyed listening to him sing and recite. "We shall return shortly."

He gently wrapped Justa's shawl around her lovely shoulders. Night air could be chilly at that time of year. Unlocking the door, he looked outside cautiously to see if anyone was lurking nearby. This cautionary behavior was a fact of life for them. They still lived with blinds drawn and doors bolted, ever mindful of the potential danger.

The happy couple strolled down the dark street in silence, at first. Then Luis said, suddenly, "Justa, my dearest, I want so desperately for you to have a good life, free from all this stress. I want this for all of us." His voice conveyed a sadness that made her heart ache. She hated seeing him depressed. Cupping his handsome face in her hands, she told him, "Do not look so grim, my love." She playfully curled a tendril of his hair in one of her fingers. "Has not Adonai protected us and delivered us from danger many times?" Her delicately sculptured features were drawn up into a questioning grimace. Her well-rounded bosom rose and fell as she spoke.

Luis could not help but notice. He had not allowed himself to become sexually involved with Justa. Embracing, kissing — yes. But, he vowed that unless he could be sure of a commitment, he would not betray her trust. His thoughts had revolved around marriage many times. He envisioned what it would be like to escape with Justa and the family to another country, to be married, to have children. However, he had made a promise to God to devote his time and energy to spreading His word, to returning as many as possible to the God of the Law of Moses. He must not be distracted. Lust was cast from his mind and his heart. It was so difficult, he conceded.

The sound of Justa's sweet voice broke into his train of thought. "...and I do love you so," she was saying. "Why can we not marry, my beloved? I want to be with you always, by you side, in your arms, in your bed. I shall be a devoted wife, Luis."

"Dear, loving Justa — do you think I am not aware of that? How can we marry now? Suppose something should happen that would force me to flee, to go into hiding? How could I desert you, my wife, and leave you in jeopardy? Please understand — I must remain free to do my work for the Almighty and, if necessary, to make sudden decisions."

"I do not care about the danger." She was weeping. Sorrowful sounds flowed from deep within her. "I want to be with you; you are my life."

Luis enveloped her in his strong arms and kissed her. *May God forgive me,* he implored, *but right now I want this woman more than anything else in the world.*

C H A P T E R   X V I I I

FEAR AND FULFILLMENT

Arturo's recent visit to Casa Chata had been productive. The friendly warden was on duty and when he approached him, the pursy fellow told him, "Manuel, Teresa, and Pedro are not fairing well." He inhaled sharply. "Manuel has already been to the torture chamber and even though he has not incriminated anyone else, the gossip is that he will break down, that he will confess after another session or two of physical agony. Poor man!"

"What about Teresa and Pedro?"

The warden exclaimed, "Unfortunate ones! They are under intense interrogation and have been threatened with the rack and the rope."

Disheartened, Arturo hastened to the de Carvajals. He was shaking with emotion as he described the covert conversation at the jail. His solemn demeanor reflected the despair they all felt. When he took his leave, he promised to keep the family apprised of any information he could gather.

Francisca and the girls were in a panic. Their tears subsided when Luis was finally able to subdue the women. All the while, his mind was racing toward a plan. It was obvious that if Manuel implicated him or any member of the family, escape from this death trap was now a priority. He vowed, whatever plan he devised, it would include his brother, the Fray Gaspar, whom he had not seen in many months. Gaspar had been relegated to the performance of mundane duties in a rural mission on the outskirts of Mexico City, since falling from grace after his arrest four years ago. Luis and Baltasar had visited him two or three times. Gaspar's discontentment with his assignment had been obvious. Now, Luis decided, was the time to save my brother's soul. It was time to bring him back to the Old Religion and to ultimate salvation. He made a mental note to see his brother as soon as possible.

For the present, however, it was imperative to contact de Silva's cousin in Vera Cruz to arrange passage aboard his ship. He hoped that Antonio was able to do this. His thoughts turned to his written memoirs and original compositions that were hidden in the ceiling of the prayer room. Luis had arranged with friends that, in the event of his rearrest, these papers should be delivered to his brothers. If he and the family were successful in fleeing to Europe, the papers were to be brought to him.

Luis could not help wondering why, after so many miraculous escapes, they should now find themselves on the brink of danger again. It must be one of the Lord's tests.

His mother's voice derailed his train of thought. "Luis, you are miles away. You are not answering me. What shall we do?"

"Dear Mother, do not worry. The Lord did not bring us out of despair to suffer at the hands of traitors. Remember, I am His shepherd and I shall lead you away from this treachery to the 'Promised Land'."

One by one, his mother and sisters kissed him goodnight and retired to their rooms. Luis sat late into the night trying to define his next step.

During the days that followed, everyone was extremely cautious. Luis choreographed the activities of his family so that no one member was ever isolated. Francisca and her daughters performed their chores and ran their errands in pairs. When Luis made his trips to Taxco on business, he called upon Antonio to keep close watch. "Antonio, make your connections," he advised one day, "for I believe it will soon be time to run for our lives."

"I shall leave for Vera Cruz as soon as possible. Do not trouble yourself. If I cannot work out something there, I shall find another way. We shall be free."

"From your mouth to God's ears," Luis repeated his mother's favorite refrain.

On Arturo's next visit, he related to the family that the attitude of the jail warden had changed. He was no longer interested in rewards for his cooperation. This news frightened them. "What does it mean? You say he even refused the ducats you offered him?" Francisca was aghast.

Arturo shrugged his shoulders and lifted his hands in resignation.

Luis intervened. "Mother, with all the arrests lately, it is obvious that the Holy Office has escalated its activities. So, evidently, they have tightened security at the jail." Inwardly, he was deeply concerned at this turn of events. How would he know what was transpiring? What of his friends? Terror gripped him — a terror he must not display. In a little while, he excused himself and went upstairs to the prayer chamber. There he fell to his knees. The supplications to Adonai were particularly intense as he prayed for strength and guidance. "Your shepherd, Oh, Lord, begs for deliverance from peril even as You delivered Daniel from the lions."

The next day was a cool, lovely one and Luis and Justa strolled through the Great Square, enjoying the outdoors. Luis expressed his anxiety about the family's anticipated flight.

"Luis, my love, my life, I shall go with you. I cannot think of living without you." Her lips were trembling.

"My beloved, you know if a sudden departure should become necessary, there would be no time…" His voice trailed off. He embraced her and kissed her wet cheeks and quivering mouth. *How dear and sweet she is…so brave*, he thought. *How can I ever part from her?* Looking at her solemn face made him regret that he had mentioned the subject. He tried to reassure her. "Perhaps I am reading too much into things. It has been many weeks since the arrests and no one has bothered us." Then, with added bravado, he said, "Surely, any day now our dear friends will be knocking at the door. So come, my darling — let us go to the café and enjoy a coffee and some sweets."

Justa patted her face with her handkerchief, dabbed at her nose, and flashed a brave but fleeting smile.

Shortly before the Christmas season of 1594, Luis planned to see some merchants in Zacatecas regarding silver bullion from the family mines. Ordinarily, he would not be away from home at this time of year because the family celebrated Hanukkah (the Celebration of the Candles), but with circumstances so unpredictable, he had to complete some cash transactions with haste.

Justa insisted, "Luis, I shall go with you. I want to take every opportunity to be with you." In spite of Luis' protests, she remained adamant.

Fear of an inquisitorial arrest had now become part of every minute of Luis' life. He would rather travel alone. With Justa along, he would have the added worry of her protection. "Please, my darling — stay with your mother. If something develops while I am on the road, I shall seek haven with friends. I do not want to expose you to possible danger."

"Dear heart, I have told you many times that you are my life, my destiny. I go!"

Luis knew better than to perpetuate the conversation. She was determined. Perhaps Clara could convince her to stay. When Luis explained the circumstances, Justa's mother pleaded with her not to go. It was of no avail.

With feet firmly planted, hands on hips, and in a voice that defied denial, Justa made it quite clear that nothing would stand in her way. She held her ground.

Luis shook his head in disbelief. The girl was incredible. He turned to Clara. "If you instruct your daughter that she may not go, I shall abide by your decision." He hoped that good judgment would triumph.

Clara looked at the two of them. Sadness overwhelmed her. She remembered how a heart could break when parting with a loved one — how it did break when that loved one never returned. *Now,* she thought, *in these terrible days, who could know what lay ahead?* Since the arrests of their friends, she feared for the de Carvajals. Clara looked at her daughter's beautiful face — now so solemn and pinched with pain. "Luis, my daughter loves you with her whole heart. If it is her choice to go, then she must. I cannot prevent it."

Her answer surprised him. *Well,* he mused, *so much for good intentions.*

They traveled by horse and wagon so that Luis could load up on the goods he was transporting. The road was often a dangerous place because of the robbers and the occasional unfriendly band of natives who roamed the woods. For the most part, Luis had a congenial relationship with the tribes in the area, thanks to his past experience in service with his uncle. It was the bandits with whom he was most concerned. Luis made sure that he always carried the necessary firearms for protection when he traveled.

After their stop in Taxco where Luis spent a few hours tying up some loose ends, it was later than he had anticipated and his concern now was seeking shelter before dark. "We must hurry, Justa. I do not want to be on the road when night falls."

Unfortunately, they were still several miles from their destination when daylight vanished and they found themselves in a heavily wooded area with no haven in sight. Soon, the road was scarcely visible. Proceeding slowly, over difficult terrain, they could hardly make out the direction of the crude path.

Justa suggested, "Let us stop for awhile, get some sleep, and, at daylight, we will continue."

"Good idea," he agreed. "Poor little one, you look so tired." Luis retrieved a blanket from behind the seat and wrapped it around her. The air was raw and chilly. "Get some rest. I will go a bit further and then take a nap, too." He put his arms around her as she cuddled up close and held the reins with his other hand. Before long, feeling weary, he decided to rest the horses and himself. He moved into the corner of the seat so as not to disturb Justa who was sound asleep.

Diane Brenda Bryan

A shrill scream pierced the air, jolting Luis to consciousness. The earliest rays of sun were penetrating the thick foliage, filtering through the branches with slivers of light. He realized the scream was Justa's, but where was she? Jumping to the ground, he grabbed the arquebus from under the seat and went in search. Almost immediately, he heard Justa scream again. Thrashing through the underbrush, he came upon a terrifying scene. Justa was engaged in a struggle with two men who were trying to force her to the ground. This is what Luis had feared: road robbers, rapists.

"Release her at once!" Luis had barely shouted the words before one of the men lunged at him with a rapier, threatening, "I will slaughter you like the pig that you are."

Finding no need to hesitate, Luis fired and the attacker fell. The other scoundrel, who was holding Justa at sword's point, turned to attack. Luis fired, accurately. A sobbing Justa clung to Luis as he comforted her with kisses and soft words. He thanked God for their safety. "Sweetheart, we shall stop soon at the inn of some good friends where we shall have some delicious food and rest awhile until you feel calm enough to travel again."

Luis blamed himself for the devastating incident. If he had not tarried in Taxco, they would have arrived, as planned, at the Casa Contento where he had spent many nights on his travels to Zacatecas. The inn was a cozy little place and the food, prepared by jolly, barrel-shaped Maria, was almost as good as his mother's — and the featherbeds were heavenly to rest upon.

Upon their arrival at Casa Contento, they were greeted with much warmth. The innkeeper Guillermo and his wife Maria were fond of Luis. They were bound in a common cause. Maria sensed, at once, that Justa was upset. When Luis described the events of the morning, the kind woman enveloped her in a motherly embrace, uttering words of consolation, that Justa responded to in a positive way.

"Come," suggested Guillermo. "You shall bathe and change your clothes and we shall partake of the wonderful meal Maria has prepared."

Maria showed them to their lodgings. Not sure of what accommodations to offer them, she showed them to adjoining rooms. The decision would rest with them, she decided, smiling mischievously. Preparing a bath for each of them, she then bustled off to the kitchen.

The meal was superb and the sparkling wine made them giddy — a welcomed change of pace. They joked and exchanged stories for awhile but, as the day drew to a close, the subject matter turned to the recent series of

133

arrests. Guillermo and Maria were distressed by the news and, although they said nothing, their faces betrayed their feelings. They told their guests, "We shall pray for your freedom and that you never fall into the hands of the Inquisition again."

"My friends," Luis said, "I place my hope in the Lord's guidance and His divine mercy."

The four of them spent long hours talking and it was not until Justa's head began to nod that Luis realized it was time to get some sleep. "Tomorrow will be a long day. We must get some rest before we start out at an early hour."

Maria promised, "But not before you have a '*desayuno grandioso*', a superb breakfast, to send you on your way."

Luis laughed. "And, '*grandioso*' it will be, for sure."

Upstairs in their rooms, Luis kissed Justa tenderly and wished her a good night's sleep. She lingered a moment and then said, in almost a whisper, "Do you realize, Luis, if you had not saved me in time, those brutes who attacked us would have taken my virginity from me?"

This totally unexpected question took Luis by surprise. He paused and then replied, in a similar, low tone of voice, "Yes, my sweet, I dread to think of you at the hands of such animals. Thank God you fought them and that I heard yours screams in time."

"Come here and take me in your arms," Justa entreated. "Your sweet tenderness will make me forget those beasts. Oh, Luis, I have such a longing for you, my love." She reached out to him. "Surely, you must feel the same, do you not?"

*God, are You testing Your servant? I have pledged my life to You and yet, this woman is my life, too. Do not suffer me to choose...*his silent words cried out.

Justa's voice interrupted his thoughts. "My beloved, can we not love Adonai and love each other, as well? I cannot believe that He would not want it so."

At that moment, neither could he. He walked to her, wrapping her in a passionate embrace. He kissed her hair, her face, her neck; he murmured every loving thought of her. His hands swept over the sensuous contours of her firm breasts and hips.

Breathing heavily, she said, in a hoarse whisper, "At last, my love, we shall know each other and be a part of each other forever."

As Luis kissed her moist, warm lips again, he gently lifted her and carried her to the bed.

CHAPTER XIX

FRUSTRATION

When Justa and Luis returned to Mexico City shortly before the holidays, they were greeted with more distressing news. Arturo was at the house when they arrived and he told them of his experience at the jail that morning. "The jailer at Casa Chata, who has been incommunicative for some time, suddenly pulled me aside and whispered, 'It is bad. Manuel has confessed to Judaizing. He has named close friends. Warrants are to be issued for more arrests. I cannot say more.' He did not even wait for his usual recompense. But, I tell you, the look on his face as he turned to go was one of compassion. I know what that look means."

Francisca and the girls fell upon Luis with entreaties. "What shall we do?" "Where can we go?" "What will happen to us?"

"Sh-sh-sh! my loved ones. I shall find Antonio and tell him to prepare for our departure as soon as possible. With the Lord's help, we shall escape from this place of torment. Have faith." To himself, he thought, *If Antonio has not arranged passage, they will have to go into hiding, seeking refuge from friends outside the city*. And, he wondered, *How long would that suffice?*

That evening, Luis hurried to his sister Catalina's house. Antonio was not at home, but Catalina informed her brother that she expected him at any moment. "He has been away on business to Vera Cruz and, I believe, he is making a stop at Puerto de los Caballos." She nodded, conspiratorially. "Meanwhile, our servants, Emilia and her husband, have been watching over us."

Luis made himself comfortable and they chatted, exchanging their innermost fears of what recent events portended. Luis pondered, "If Antonio has not or cannot arrange immediate passage, I am not sure what course we shall be forced to resort to. But, this I know — we must leave here as soon as possible."

Catalina had never seen her brother so agitated, at least, not since their arrests five years ago. Even then, he had maintained his strength and determination and he had saved the family. It hurt her to see the suffering in his eyes; he looked as if all resistance had been drained from him.

A sudden sound at the door startled them. They almost bolted out of their seats when a familiar voice called out, "My wife, where are you?"

"In the sitting room, Antonio," she responded, with relief. "Luis is here with me."

"Un momento," he called back as he hastened up the stairs to his daughter's room. The child was asleep so Antonio kissed her lovingly on both cheeks, hoping not to wake her. She stirred briefly and murmured, "Hello, Papa" and promptly fell back to sleep.

Antonio came down the stairs slowly, dreading to face Luis. He kissed his wife and embraced his brother-in-law. He told his wife to bring some wine. To Luis, he said, "I am afraid I have bad news. I tried to arrange passage with de Silva's cousin but, unfortunately, he explained to me that he would not be leaving for another month. The papers for his ship have been processed, but he is to sail with the flota to Europe next month." His heart ached as he watched the impact of these words upon Luis.

"You know we cannot wait a month. Everything is closing in around us." Luis' deeply furrowed brows betrayed the internal turmoil, the struggle to cope with this disappointment. The expression on his face was one of unspeakable sorrow.

"I was so sure I could help. Now?" Antonio felt the frustration rising within him. "I shall find a way!" he shouted, as his fist inadvertently crashed down on the little table nearby.

"Do not distress yourself, my brother. You did your best." Luis patted him on the back. Then lifting his arms upward — a gesture Antonio interpreted to mean hopelessness — Luis declared, in a fervent voice, "The Lord will guide me in His wondrous ways and I shall find the right path. Pray for another miracle, my loved ones. Keep hope alive in your hearts." He kissed them both and left.

Antonio took Catalina into his arms. "Your brother's faith is his armor. He is truly a soldier of God."

For several days, Luis meditated and prayed, barely eating, sublimating all his desires to prayer and communication with God. One night, he had a dream that profoundly affected him. He saw himself walking in a green field that was alive with patches of brilliantly-hued flowers. Amidst this loveliness sat his father on a velvet chair, the frame of which was gilded, and next to him on a throne sat the Lord. Luis' father smiled and beckoned to him and Adonai welcomed him. The dream then ended abruptly but when Luis awakened, he understood God's plan and accepted it.

Justa had been to the house several times since their return but she had seen Luis only once. He spent all his time in the prayer chamber and nothing, not even his love for Justa, could deter him. Finally, during Hanukkah, Francisca insisted that Luis have a meal with the family. She invited Justa to join them. Under the circumstances, it was not the usual, happy celebration. Conversation was sparse. After the meal, Luis and Justa went out back to the little sitting area near Francisca's vegetable garden to enjoy the serenity and loveliness. Luis took Justa's hand in his. "I am sorry, my dearest, that I have not been more attentive to you, but the situation is a dangerous one. This is exactly what I feared might happen. My every thought is now consumed with escape."

Justa gently caressed his face. Her dainty fingers lingered a moment around his lips as she bent forward to kiss them. "I understand, my love. Do not worry for my sake. I will face whatever lies in store and deal with it. I am strong, more so even now because of our love. At least, my darling, we have enjoyed compete fulfillment. I shall cherish those precious moments forever."

He held her tightly as he kissed her and said sadly, "My darling, you will be in my heart as long as I live — and after that." They stood there in a quiet embrace for several minutes until Luis suggested, "The night grows damp. Let us rejoin the others."

Almost two months had elapsed since Manuel's arrest. The security around the jail had increased again and Arturo was not able to get any information from the warden, in spite of some tempting offers. Once again, the usually jovial fellow now seemed aloof and preoccupied. Arturo could not fathom these changes in his behavior. He had no awareness of the new restrictions imposed upon the jailers or he would have understood. The inquisitors had issued a prohibitive warning against conversing with prisoners and visitors. They had decreed it to be a punishable offense.

It was only after Manuel had suffered four intense interrogations and two trips to the torture chamber that he broke down, naming — among others — Luis de Carvajal. He confessed to Judaizing and proselytizing and spoke of Luis as an honored and revered teacher. The inquisitors, adept in their profession, and having the advantage of information gleaned during the previous arrests of the family, were able to elicit and direct damaging evidence against them.

The longer the questioning and the torture, the more deeply did Manuel sink into an abyss of total incrimination and, along with him, like a swirling tidal current, a myriad of dear friends were swept away into the madness that was the Inquisition.

The Holy Office was on the verge of a big coup because of the recent testimonies. It was already formulating a plan for an impressive *auto-da-fe* and took the necessary precautions that not even the slightest bit of information leaked out which might aid and abet those under surveillance. Forewarned is forearmed, and by this code of silence the inquisitors hoped to eliminate any possibility of escape. Meanwhile, the Holy Office continued its investigations of assets and properties of those scheduled to be taken into custody.

The prospect of re-arresting the de Carvajals gave Alonso de Peralta great satisfaction. He was certain that Luis' potential as a leader of the Secret Jews was a threat to all that believed in Jesus Christ. Hatred consumed the inquisitor. If the intelligence provided by Manuel de Lucena was accurate then Luis, the heretic, had no future. Peralta decided, however, that he would not rely on Manuel's testimony alone. This time he wanted irrefutable and conclusive evidence. He reflected on Luis' first arrest, five years ago, when Luis had abjured "de vehementi," giving his promise, in writing, to reconcile with the church and never to return to the God of the Law of Moses. This time, Peralta swore, he would make sure that there would be no opportunity to save Luis or his family.

He sent for his secretary. "Where is the list of recently admitted prisoners? Please bring it to me," he instructed. "There must be some who are acquainted with the de Carvajals and, no doubt, worshipped in secret with them — the blasphemers!"

The secretary hurried away to get the information for the inquisitor. Within a short time, he returned with the latest postings. Peralta thanked and dismissed him. As he browsed through the list, he decided to embark upon a vigorous campaign to methodically destroy the family. It would take time but the prize would be worth the effort.

On January 3, 1595, Inquisitor Peralta ordered that Lorenzo Vargas be brought before him. He had chosen Vargas from the list because he observed that the boy was a neighbor of the de Carvajals. Peralta noted to his colleagues, with sinister humor, "This might be just the person to add more fuel to the fire."

Lorenzo Vargas was a tall, gangly lad of twenty-one years. Curly, ebony hair framed a pleasant face, embellished by flushed cheeks and moist, dark eyes which displayed an almost childlike innocence. At this moment, he stood quaking before his interrogator. Lorenzo had heard the horror stories of arrests by the Holy Office. He was not told why he had been apprehended. They had approached him while he was peddling his wares in the city, two weeks ago.

At a signal, the clerk began swearing in the witness. "Under solemn oath, do you swear that all you will say at this audience and any future audience will be the truth?"

"Yes, yes, I do, I swear," the youth answered anxiously.

"And do you further swear not to speak of anything you hear or see at these proceedings to anyone?"

"Yes, I do — I swear."

Peralta again took charge. "What is your name, age and place of birth?"

"My name is Lorenzo Vargas. I am twenty-one years old and I was born in Mogodura, Portugal."

"What is your occupation?"

"I am a peddler. I sell fabrics, threads, dyes and other sewing accessories."

"Who are your parents?"

"My father is Simon Vargas, a tanner by trade, and my mother, Rosa, is a seamstress. To the best of my knowledge, they are alive and still reside in Mogodura."

The next series of questions concerned his grandparents, uncles, and aunts. Lorenzo provided as many details as he could recall; however, there was much that he did not know except for some names, occupations, and places of residences.

"When did you arrive in Mexico City?" Peralta asked, now focusing on Lorenzo again.

Disjointed thoughts whirled inside the boy's head. He wished he knew why he was there. They had told him nothing. His goods had been confiscated and he had been hauled off to Casa Chata. Did they suspect? The stern voice of the inquisitor broke into his pondering. Lorenzo recoiled at the harshness of its sound and the coldness of the penetrating eyes.

"You are not answering, boy. Stop trembling!" he ordered. Then moderating his tone, he suggested, "Tell me about your arrival here. When was that?"

The youth composed himself. "About a year ago, sir. I came over with the flota in the Spring of 1594."

"How was it you came alone? Did no one else from your family accompany you?"

"No, no one There were many stories about the opportunities in New Spain. It was decided that I should try my luck and, if all went well, my family would join me later."

"With whom and where do you reside?"

"I was given a room by the de Marco family in their house on Avenido de la Fe. A relative in Mogodura suggested that I contact the de Marcos upon my arrival, which I did. They were kind enough to offer me shelter."

The inquisitor made a notation in his file to check the de Marco family. Perhaps there is more here than meets the eye. "Are you acquainted with your neighbors, Lorenzo?"

"Yes, I am. There are the de Carvajals on one side, and the Rodriquez' on the other."

"Tell me about them. Are they good neighbors? Good Christians?"

Lorenzo's guard went up at once. Now he knew where all this was leading. Another witch hunt. The tales of imprisoned and tortured victims raced around in his head. He began to sweat. His nemesis, well aware of the impact of his question, made a magnanimous gesture in an attempt to quell Lorenzo's panic, which was now apparent.

"My dear boy, do not be upset. Just answer my questions to the best of your ability." He paused, then continued, "Tell me about your neighbors, the de Carvajals. Do they go to church on Sundays?"

Lorenzo quickly affirmed, "Yes, they do. I attend the same church and they are always there. Fray Pedro visits with them often."

Ah, yes, Fray Pedro, Peralta ruminated, *the old friar at the Colegia to which Luis had been assigned. I often wonder about him — his closeness to the family and his fondness of them, especially Luis. There are times when I sense the friar's disapproval of inquisitorial procedures. Yet, I cannot put my finger on it precisely.* He turned to Lorenzo again. "What do you do on Saturdays?"

"I peddle my goods. You can check with the man who arrested me. It was on a Saturday." He felt this was significant to prove it was not a day he observed.

"Do you ever see your neighbors on Saturdays? Do they work as well?"

Lorenzo answered apologetically, "I really do not take notice of anything except getting ready for my work. I like to get an early start." He was as evasive as possible and he could see the muscles hardening in his questioner's face. This frightened him.

There was a prolonged silence while Peralta sat motionless, staring at the prisoner. Suddenly, Peralta stood up, declared the audience over, and remanded Lorenzo back to his cell. Nothing more than that. Lorenzo tried to comprehend the meaning of this abrupt dismissal. The jailers held him by each arm and led him out.

Peralta sat back in his chair. His smile was wicked and insidious and reflected the malice of his intent. *The youth was thoroughly intimidated*, he reasoned. *Perhaps some time alone in his cell and a little 'persuasion' would refresh his memory.*

One evening, when Luis returned from a trip to Taxco, his neighbor Senor Marco pulled him aside and told him of Lorenzo's arrest. He could not understand why the boy had been apprehended and asked if Luis could look into the matter. This he promised to do.

Luis' concern now multiplied. This was a most hapless turn of events. The family had befriended Lorenzo and, when Luis learned that he was a New Christian, he gradually influenced him to return to the Old Religion. Often, the lad would join them at their secret prayer meetings. The de Marcos, devout Old Christians, knew nothing of this.

Luis went at once to his sister's house in search of Antonio. Luckily, he was at home. "Antonio, they have arrested the Vargas boy."

"Yes, I know," he answered. "I just heard about it from Arturo."

"I feel like a vise is tightening around us and will soon crush the life out of the de Carvajals." Luis' tone was one of desperation.

"You are right to be concerned. We have had no news for several weeks about Manuel, Teresa, or Pedro. We can only imagine the worst. And now this? Do you think Lorenzo has the courage and stamina to stand up to those brutes?"

"God give him strength," Luis implored.

CHAPTER XX

DISCLOSURE

Six months had passed since Lorenzo's incarceration. Never had he felt such desolation and despair. The misery of the moist, dreary cell penetrated his body and soul. An indictment had been handed down against him for the crime of having knowledge of Judaizers and not reporting them. No accusations had been made against him as a "Judaizante."

Peralta had decided that this modified charge would suffice for the time being. Prisoners were more inclined to talk freely if they thought it would prevent them from being charged with more stringently punishable crimes.

In June, Lorenzo was informed that he was scheduled to appear before a general tribunal on July 1st, to be formally charged. The prelate who came to his cell with the news sat and spoke with the unhappy prisoner. "Son, you have nothing to fear if you tell the truth the way you swore to do. You will be treated accordingly."

This was no consolation to Lorenzo. The truth would not set him free. "Padre, I have done nothing wrong. I do not understand about reporting Judaizers."

"My son, tell the Tribunal all you know and they will be merciful." The priest blessed him and left. On his way out of the jail, he had the uneasy feeling that the actions of the Inquisition were not what the Lord Jesus Christ would condone.

During what seemed an interminable time alone in his cell, the only voices Lorenzo heard were whispered remarks outside his door and, too often, the screams and pleadings of the tortured. These tore at his soul. *This place*, he thought, *was hell on earth*. Many times he wished himself dead rather than face the prospect of pain and suffering — or worse.

One morning, the waiting came to an end. Two jailers came to his cell and informed him that this was the day of his second audience. They permitted him to wash and put on clean attire they provided. While they waited for Lorenzo, the jailers expressed pity for this young and vulnerable youth.

Walking toward the building, Lorenzo softly murmured a prayer and, for a little while, he sensed a calmness come over him. Sadly, the feeling did not last long. When the jailers ushered him into that chamber of cold stone, he saw several robed figures at a long table upon which stood three lighted candelabra. The flickering of the candles cast eerie shadows upon the walls. Lorenzo could not resist the thought that the dark images resembled demons, and this was hell, was it not? A familiar voice jarred his reverie. It was Peralta's. Lorenzo had hoped that someone else might be questioning him this time. But, he reasoned, maybe that would have been worse, who knows.

The secretary of the court sat on the side, ready to begin the proceedings and to record them. The swearing in finished and the charges read, the inquisitor resumed his interrogation. "Lorenzo, you have spent many months alone in your cell. Have you re-examined your memory? Perhaps you will be able to provide us with some information pertinent to the work of the Holy Office."

The prisoner answered, "I shall try, to the best of my recollection." Sheer dread enveloped him.

"If you will recall, during your first interrogation I asked you about your neighbors — if they were good Christians and if they worked on Saturdays, the way you did. You seemed to have trouble answering and your response was unsatisfactory. You said you did not notice what your neighbors did because you left for work so early in the morning."

"But that is so. That is the truth," Lorenzo insisted.

Peralta became enraged. "I warn you — I will not tolerate any more evasion. If necessary, we can stretch your memory on the rack and the ropes."

This statement caused Lorenzo to gasp. He had heard about the rack and the ropes from conversations between the jailers and, the sounds from the torture chamber.

Peralta continued, "Tell me, Lorenzo — did you ever have a meal with the de Carvajals? What did they serve?"

"Yes, I had dinner with them on several occasions. Mostly on Friday nights. Senora Francisca usually served a 'roz con pollo'. Chicken and rice — delicious," he added, and then caught himself. That was a sweet memory, but he could not afford to linger in it.

What was Peralta leading up to, he wondered. The next question clarified his intentions. "How did Senora de Carvajal prepare the chicken before cooking it? Did you ever observe her slaughter a chicken or did she buy one already killed?"

The youth swallowed hard before he answered. "One day, I did see her in the kitchen with a live chicken in hand. She ordered her servant to decapitate it, salt it, and let the blood drain. Then the fowl was thoroughly washed. Senora de Carvajal said she had received the live chicken as a gift." Lorenzo knew full well that Francisca preferred to butcher fowl and prepare meat according to Jewish custom. He had heard her tell her servant once when she had asked him to cut the jugular vein of a lamb first, that this method of butchering helped the meat to stay fresh longer.

For his part, Peralta recognized the procedure as that of Judaizers. In the Dead Law of Moses, he recalled, in Genesis 9:4 and Leviticus 7:26, the consuming of blood of bird or animal to be eaten is specifically forbidden. The inquisitor tapped his fingers on the table. *Well,* he thought, *now we are finally getting somewhere.* "Did you ever notice anything about the dress habits of Luis de Carvajal or other members of the family? Were there times when they wore the finest rather than their everyday attire?"

The accused hesitated. He felt like an animal caught in a trap. On Fridays, the family was involved in preparing for the Sabbath — the cleanliness of the house and personal hygiene were attended to. At the dinner table, all were dressed in their finery. Lorenzo had always made sure that he was presentable, in clean clothes and with facial hair properly trimmed.

A shout from Peralta clipped his thoughts. "Stop dreaming, Senor Vargas. Answer!"

"Sir, everyone always looked nice. But is it not customary for people to put a little more emphasis on how they dress when guests are coming?" The trap was tightening for him, he realized.

"Lorenzo Vargas, I warn you — you are one step away from having your tongue loosened."

"Well," he stammered, "they were dressed in fine clothes that I never noticed on other days."

Peralta had the answer he wanted. He changed course. "What time do you return home on Saturdays?"

"About four o'clock, Sir."

"Did you ever stop in to visit the de Carvajals on a Saturday, after work? "Yes. Once or twice. I do not like to impose."

"I understand. That is not a convenient time to visit. No doubt, that is when the Senora is preparing dinner. Was she, indeed, doing that at any time when you stopped in on Saturdays?"

Hedging, Lorenzo answered, "She could have been. I did not notice. She would chat with me for awhile and then I would leave."

"Tell the truth. Was there any sign of activity in the kitchen? Were any of the daughters cooking? Perhaps the odor of food was noticeable. Was the table set?" Peralta's voice rose with every question, which came with lightning speed and did not permit Lorenzo time to answer. When the inquisitor shrieked, "You will not see the light of day again if I do not get some answers," it had a paralyzing affect upon its recipient.

Lorenzo admitted, "No, I saw no sign of preparing for dinner on any Saturday, nor was the table set. Francisca and her daughters were in the sitting room, relaxing." What was left unspoken was the fact that food prepared on Friday sufficed for the Saturday meal because lighting the stove or any kind of work was not permitted on the Sabbath. After sundown, regular activities were resumed. He had enjoyed these late afternoons with the de Carvajals. Now? He shuddered to think.

Peralta's voice again, asking, "Did they offer you a coffee or anything to eat or drink?"

"No, sir."

"That was not hospitable, was it? They feed you a good dinner on a Friday night but not even a coffee the next afternoon?" Peralta relished every moment, watching Lorenzo squirm.

The unhappy youth hunched his shoulders and made a feeble attempt to say something but, before he could reply, Peralta turned away from him, made more notations in his folder and said, "Enough for today. Perhaps next time you will be of greater assistance." Actually, he was satisfied that Lorenzo had already provided enough damaging evidence. He ordered the jailers to take the prisoner back to the jail.

A crestfallen Lorenzo was led out of the building. He was grateful for the few breaths of fresh air he enjoyed on his way back to Casa Chata.

Dr. Lobo Guerrero and Licentiate Alonso de Peralta met with the prosecuting attorney, Dr. Martos de Bohorques, to discuss the Lorenzo Diego case. After exchanging opinions on the value of the testimony given during his two audiences, they determined that in order to expedite things, they would recommend a few "turns of the rope" rather than go to the trouble of holding a third audience with Lorenzo. Guerrero and Peralta would both be present in the torture chamber, it was decided, to hear any confession made by the boy.

This decision effected an amazing result. After one or two turns of the rope, the unlucky prisoner cried out for mercy and agreed to divulge any information they wanted. The recorder was on hand to take notes. Lorenzo confessed to attending prayer meetings at the de Carvajals, after dinner, on Friday nights, and also on other occasions. "I did so only because I felt obligated. The family had befriended me. I myself am a devout Christian. I did not allow anything they said to sway me."

"Can you supply the names of others who attended these meetings?"

Lorenzo named several people, among them Justa Mendez.

"Well done, my son." Peralta complimented the tearful, suffering prisoner.

"Will I be able to go home soon?" he asked. "I have told you all I know. In the torture chamber, you assured me of my freedom if I cooperated."

Peralta retorted, "There is some clerical work to be done. It will take some time. You will hear from us when we have made our final determination." The inquisitor thought, *It is best to keep him incarcerated, out of reach of friends, for the time being.* He continued, "Meanwhile, as a reward, we shall move you to a different cell which you will find more comfortable — one with a window."

Peralta gave the order for the jailers to take Lorenzo to his new accommodations. Then he turned to Dr. Guerrero. "That is the least we can do for him, eh?" He smirked. "Such a fountain of facts!"

CHAPTER XXI

SEIZURE

The Holy Office moved swiftly. Everything was in place for the coup de grace. The files were brimming with 'confessions' that made their case indisputable. All the facts pointed to an irrefutable accusation of *Judaizante relapso pertinaz* against Luis de Carvajal, el mozo — an accusation that he had relapsed to the Old Religion.

"Now," Peralta told Guerrero, "it is time for the last card trick."

It was the morning of March 1, 1595, and Francisca arose earlier than usual because Luis, who had spent most of the night in prayer, had called to her. "Mother dear, will you join me for breakfast? I want to discuss something with you."

"With pleasure, my son," she called back. Sleep was almost a stranger to her. The whole family lived in a state of apprehension since Arturo related what he had heard at the jail. Francisca dressed hurriedly and joined her son.

In moments, a platter of fruit and some bread and cheese were on the table, complemented by a pot of brewed coffee. Francisca was fearful of what her son might say to her. Every evening she listened to his supplications to the Lord, asking for another miracle. What little hope they had was slipping away like sand through their fingers.

"Mother, when Arturo brought us the awful news, that same night I had a dream that I believe is guidance from Adonai." Luis described the vision. "I think I know what God wants of me. He has shown me that there is a place for me in Heaven and that I shall find salvation. Blessed be the Lord who complies with our worthy desires."

Francisca was in tears. "We must get away. My beloved Luis, I would give my life to save yours. What can I do?" she implored, wringing her hands in utter despair.

They sat there looking at each other, their hearts heavy, devoid of hope. Luis tried to cheer her up with a smile and a big hug. He kissed her cheek. "I love you, Mother. Remember that God is showing mercy, not only for me but also for you and my sisters. Meanwhile, be comforted by the thought that He will perform another miracle. You will see."

A loud knock at the door startled them. What could it mean at this early hour? It was just barely dawn. Terror gripped Francisca as she approached the door and asked, "Who is there, *por favor?*"

A loud, gruff voice demanded, "Open this door, at once. We are emissaries from the Holy Office."

With a look of resignation, Luis signaled her to let them in. She hesitated. Another rough, unfriendly, "Open the door, I tell you!" and Francisca complied. When she let them in, she was pushed aside. The warden and the commissary were there to arrest Luis. As they lunged at him, she cried out in anguish, "My son, my son!" She was cautioned to be quiet.

"Luis de Carvajal, *el Mozo,* you are under arrest by order of the High Tribunal of the Inquisition of Mexico City," the warden loudly proclaimed. He grabbed for Luis, who shrugged him off momentarily to comfort his weeping mother. They kissed each other, murmuring hopes for his safe return. He held her briefly in an embrace and whispered, "Remember, have faith, be strong. God is with us."

The warden pulled Luis away and led him toward the door. "Come along and do not make any trouble," he warned. "You are in enough already."

As they led him away from the house, Luis looked back and saw that his mother was now flanked by two of his sisters. The girls had awakened when they heard the commotion. They rushed down the stairs in time to see their brother being taken away, under arrest. Just before climbing into the open wagon, he shouted to them, "Be brave. Believe."

Within minutes, Francisca was hurrying to Antonio's house. When she told him what had transpired, he decided to take the family Acapulco as soon as possible. It was their only chance. He would smuggle them aboard a ship sailing for Macao with the Asian fleet. There was a captain who was a close friend; he would help. Meanwhile, he had to get them out of Mexico City. He sent Francisca home and hastened to Arturo's house. Antonio awakened him, explained the situation, and told him, "You must get Francisca and the girls to Acapulco. I will ride ahead to see what I can arrange — pay off some people in the right places — anything — we <u>must</u> save them. There is no time to be lost. Soon there will be another knock at the door."

"I understand," Arturo said. "Tell me what I must do."

Antonio outlined his plan. "Hire two wagons and ask Nazareo to drive one; you will drive the other. He can be trusted. His wife Emilia and he have been with the family for years. Make sure you have enough provisions and be careful not to arouse any suspicion. Instruct the family to take only those things that they can carry. If anyone stops you and asks questions, tell them nothing, if possible. If you must answer, make up some story about visiting relatives in a nearby town."

He gave Arturo some money and a firm handshake. "Go with God, cousin." Arturo clasped his arms around Antonio and then hastened away to follow his instructions. As Antonio watched him go, he agonized, *If only I had not waited.* When he was unsuccessful at Vera Cruz, he had formulated a plan for Acapulco but had not finalized the actual passages, therefore, he had delayed discussing it with Luis. He beat his chest now, in frustration, and wailed, "Why did I not speak up? I had so wanted to surprise them with some good news, some hope, and now look at what has happened. Only a few more day, perhaps, and it could have been accomplished. Oh, God — why did I wait?"

Now, he thought, *poor Luis is in the hands of the devils and God only knows if the rest of the family will arrive safely in Acapulco. If they do, will I be successful in getting them aboard a ship?* He had left funds with Uncle Hector and instructed him to pay for any available passage. The captain who had befriended Antonio in the past had carried many Secret Jews aboard his ship to and from Asia, and Antonio was relying upon his help.

There was no time to lose. He saddled his horse and prepared for the ride to Acapulco, but first he must bring his wife to her mother's house. He would leave her there and bring his daughter Leonor and his niece Anica to a safe haven. Their best place right now would be with Emilia, who had been Leonor's nanny from birth. She would care for the children at her house until his return from Acapulco. Thank God, the Inquisition showed no interest in him. His impeccable posture as a Catholic and his connections with the right people helped — even if it did cost him "*mucho dinero.*" Should something go wrong at Acapulco, at least the little ones would be safe here. Then he would plan his and the children's escape. It was not easy to leave Catalina with her mother and take the children away. Their tearful farewells were heartbreaking. "Only for a little while, my darlings," both mothers tried to assure the little girls, whose sorrowful demeanors reflected the depths of their confusion and despair.

Antonio pulled his wife aside, stroking her cheeks and kissing her fervently. "Be brave, my love. The Lord hears the prayers of those who love Him and He shall watch over you. We shall all be together soon, on our way to freedom."

"Adios, my husband. God be with you and the children."

He turned away. He could not bear to see their sorrow, nor did he want them to see his. He whispered, "God be with you, too," and walked quickly out of the house with the children.

The parting at Emilia's house was a sad one. The children cried and stood there clutching him, asking why he had to go. When he told them he was going to make plans for a trip for the whole family, it allayed their fears somewhat. Emilia gave them some sweets and sang a little song they always enjoyed together. She promised the girls, "Do not worry, little ones. Emilia will keep you safe until Senor Antonio returns."

He pressed some money into her hand and said, "I shall return as soon as possible. Thank you and God bless you."

"And you, sir," Emilia answered.

Antonio's instructions to her were explicit. The safety of the children was a priority. She was to maintain a low profile, keeping her wards indoors most of the time in order to avoid the curiosity of neighbors. It had been customary for Emilia to care for the children for a day or two, but not for an extended period. She wondered how long it would be before the Senor returned. No matter. This faithful nanny would guard the children with her life, if necessary, she pledged.

Antonio went directly to the stables. It would be a long, hard ride to Acapulco. Quickly gathering some essentials, he rode off, disappearing into the outlying districts of Mexico City. It would be a tedious trip and he would have to ride at a fast pace, ever careful not to arouse anyone's interest. Riding at a feverish pace, he prayed that Uncle Hector had made a deal with the captain. All he could think about was the solemn parting with the family and the children.

He rode the rest of the day, into the evening, stopping only for a quick repast and a beverage. It was urgent that he get to Uncle Hector's before Arturo and Nazareo. He prayed that his captain friend would be in port getting a ship ready. The Asian fleet was due to leave soon.

An exhausted rider approached the door of the familiar house. His uncle embraced Antonio and made him welcome. "My nephew, it is good to see you again." Then cautiously, he added, "You are not in any trouble, are you?"

Antonio explained the situation — the arrest of Luis and the plight of the others and his plan to help.

A distressed Hector promised, "I shall help in any way possible. Your friend, the captain, has his ship in readiness for departure. I saw the preparations going on when I went down to the dock this morning and alerted him to the possibility of passengers. Go at once, Antonio, and make plans with him."

"Yes, Uncle, I shall do so and return shortly. Thank you."

Antonio loved the briny smell and the coarse sounds of the harbor. At the dock, he found a sailor busy at work and asked for directions to the Senora de Espana. The sailor indicated a vessel close by. The ship was being loaded according to directions given by a man obviously in authority. Antonio tiptoed up behind him, poking him in the back, saying, "Good evening, *camarada*."

The startled captain whirled around. "Ah, it is you de Caceres. Thank God." He sighed with relief. "One never knows, these days who is tapping you on the back. Are the Senora de Carvajal and her daughters here? Hector told me to expect them."

"No, not yet, but they should arrive within the next twenty-four hours or sooner."

"Good. We sail Sunday morning."

The two men chatted a while longer, exchanging information and instructions. "Many thanks, my friend," Antonio said when he took his leave. He hastened back to the house to wait — and pray.

The next day, Friday, dragged on in a tedious procession of hours and Hector and Antonio could barely contain their emotions. Conversations ran the gamut from optimism to dejection. "If only we had some way of knowing whether all was going according to plan with the travelers," Hector said. At this point in time, they could do nothing but continue their vigil. They spent an endless day and evening playing cards and reminiscing. The uncle tried to amuse his nephew with anecdotes about his childhood in Portugal and Antonio talked of his life in Mexico City. Ever so often there would be a rift in the conversation, their eyes welling up, their voices choking up, their words barely audible.

After they both had retired, the sounds of snorting horses and the muffled voices of weary travelers awakened them. Hector jumped from his bed, donned a cloak over his nightshirt, and ran outside to greet his relatives. "Thank the Lord — you are here safe and sound." He could hardly contain his excitement and the relief he felt.

Right behind him, Antonio charged up to the wagons. Nazareo was helping Francisca and the girls. A happy Antonio grabbed the women, swinging them about, one at a time. Then he fiercely hugged his beloved Catalina, who teased, "You are squeezing the breath out of me, my dear." Her laugh was like tinkling piano notes.

"I cannot help myself. I am so overjoyed to see you, my dearest, and to see all my loved ones."

Antonio shook hands with Arturo and Nazareo, thanking them profusely for delivering their precious 'cargo' safely. He asked, "How was the trip? Any problems?"

"We would have been here sooner but there were necessary stops. You understand — the ladies —" Arturo stuttered a bit, embarrassed by the explanation.

Hector and Antonio laughed.

"Also," continued Arturo, "we did not want to attract any attention by displaying any urgency, so our pace was slower than it could have been. There was much activity on the road. We thought it best not to show haste."

Antonio praised them. "Well done, my comrades."

The old Negro smiled when Arturo indicated that he could not have accomplished the escape without his help. "Nazareo was a fine man to have along."

They enjoyed some coffee and sandwiches with details of their trip overflowing in rapid succession. Francisca would not allow anyone to go to bed until they had all joined in a prayer of gratitude. As they recited thanks to the Lord, all were painfully aware of Luis' absence. The only consolation Antonio could offer was that when he returned to Mexico City, he would do all in his power to secure Luis' freedom. His allies were his money and property, and he would offer them to the Holy Office. He vowed, "Luis will not be sacrificed."

The next day, everyone was in a state of heightened excitement but as the time drew near for their departure, the painful realization that they were leaving Luis behind became unbearable, especially for Francisca. It took a lot of persuasion to get her to agree to go. Antonio swore that they would be united again because he would pay off the proper authorities. At first adamant, Francisca insisted that she would stay with Hector until Luis' fate was known. At last, persuasion prevailed and, with great reluctance, she consented to go.

They all knew that the re-arrest of a Secret Jew who had formerly reconciled with the Church and "abjured de vehementi" was automatically subject to retrial by the Inquisition and when sentenced the recommendation would be death at the stake — the *quemadero*. Antonio maintained a positive flow of conversation and encouraged the family to retreat to a position of acceptance and utmost optimism. God's will shall prevail.

Sunday finally dawned. All were prepared for the journey. As they prepared to go to the dock, Antonio thought it best to say his goodbyes at the house and get an early start back to Mexico City. He instructed his uncle, "You will escort my precious ones to the ship and give the good Captain this additional money, as agreed. I shall expect news from you through Arturo and Nazareo, who will leave for Mexico City as soon as the ship leaves port."

"Certainly, nephew. You should have some news within a few days. Godspeed!"

As Antonio rode off, words of love followed him on the early morning air.

The scene at the docks, as usual, was a tumultuous one. Sailors were scurrying about, officers were shouting orders, passengers inquiring about their transports and then hastening to them — bundles, boxes, and bags in hand — and merchants making last minute checks to ascertain that their cargoes were loaded and accounted for.

Hector and the family walked slowly from the far corner of the wharf toward the Senora de Espana which stood majestically waiting as the sea rolled in with waves which lapped against her hulk. It was early but already the sky was wiping away the cobwebs and soon the sun shone down upon them from a clear, bright expanse of azure. *So far, everything is going according to plan*, Hector thought. He was thankful and relieved. The women would soon be on their way to freedom. Francisca carried with her a letter to a dear friend of his in Macao who would provide shelter for them. There they would wait until Antonio arrived with the children — and with Luis, please, God!

The captain stood at the foot of the gangplank. He could see the family approaching and he looked forward not only to helping them but to the extra money he had been promised. He lifted his arm and waved them forward. Hector and the women quickened their steps.

Suddenly, two black-caped figures in broad brimmed black hats stepped abruptly in front of them. "By order of the Holy Office of Mexico City, the following people are to be apprehended and brought before the High Tribunal to face charges made against them: Francisca de Carvajal and her daughters, Isabel, Leonor, Catalina, and Mariana."

155

Upon his return from Acapulco, Antonio rushed to Emilia's house. Thank God, the children were safe! Emilia told him that the little news she had was whatever she could glean from her brother who worked at Casa Chata, delivering the trays of food to the prisoners. Sadly, she told him, "Luis, poor man, has been subjected to torture. He seemed to be holding fast, but now I hear he has suffered so intensely, enough to give himself up and also the names of many others."

Antonio asked, "Is the Warden Alejandro still working there? I must see if I can get a message to Luis."

"As far as I know, he is. I saw him the other day. I can stop by, if you wish. Nobody will think anything of it. If you give me the message, my brother will see to it that Alejandro delivers it."

"Good." Antonio hurriedly wrote a cryptic note and signed it with the pseudonym "Gregorio", a name they had agreed he would assume in times of extreme caution. Luis would know that he is there and will help. He slipped some money into an envelope with the note, thanked Emilia, and left with the children.

On the way home, the little girls chattered and asked many questions, especially about their mother and aunts. He explained how they were on a ship going to Macao and that soon they, too, would leave to join the rest of the family. This appeased the children. To change the course of the conversation, he suggested, "Come, let us buy something for dinner."

At the *plaza de mercado*, the marketplace, they purchased some meat and vegetables. "Now," said Antonio, "I shall buy you some delicious surprises." He took them to the pastry shop, where he conversed briefly with his friend, the baker, and purchased cookies and a bag of candies that he knew the children preferred.

At home, after dinner, they obediently waited for their surprises. "I have your favorite cookies and chocolates," Antonio tempted, "but, first, a big hug and kiss from each of you." The children obliged, squealing with delight in anticipation. He looked at them, his heart full of love and pain, and envied their ability to be swayed from fear and uncertainty by the promise of sweets. In the days to come, he feared, even that will wear itself thin until he can complete his plan for escape. There are only so many cookies, so much chocolate…He sighed and then smiled at them. "Come little ones, let us enjoy."

Later that same night, Arturo and Nazareo returned to Mexico City and hastened to Antonio's house to tell him of the unfortunate turn of events on the dock at Acapulco. A feeling of foreboding filled Antonio as he went to answer the late knock at the door. "Who is there, please?"

"Arturo. Open the door, Antonio." It was the urgency in his voice that made the blood in Antonio's veins momentarily halt its course. He sensed that something had gone awry. The two men rushed in. Arturo's face was contorted and agitated and he was trembling.

"What has happened? Tell me," Antonio urged.

Arturo tearfully described the scene at the ship. Antonio collapsed in a chair nearby. All he could do was cry out, "Why, God, why now? They were so close. Why?"

CHAPTER XXII

RETURN TO PURGATORY

When Luis arrived at Casa Chata, he was immediately thrown into one of the secret dungeons. It was no stranger to him, nor he to it. After a day and night of anguished prayer, he was surprised to hear the jailer's voice call to him from outside his door. "Luis, I have brought a cell mate for you."

The iron hinges grated as the heavy door swung open and a man was shoved into the chamber. Luis heard the bolt drop back into place after the door closed. There was no window and only a flickering candle provided dim light. Luis peered into the semi-darkness and asked, "Who are you?" He lifted the candle and held it up between them, aware now of the familiar black frock worn by the stranger.

"I am Carlos Diaz, a priest — one who has gotten into a little trouble, I am afraid." His voice displayed concern, yet he smiled warmly at Luis.

Luis wondered if this priest would turn out to be a friend and confidante the way Friar de Luna had and who, he fondly recalled, had become a convert to Judaism. He asked, "What sort of trouble are you in, padre?"

"Some little transgression in the confessional — you know." He winked broadly at Luis.

Luis thought, *Some little flirtation, perhaps a little more...Whatever it was, the padre will feel only a slight sting of the inquisitors.* He nodded and said nothing.

During the next few hours, Luis did not converse with Diaz. Instead, he put on his hat and coat and knelt in prayer, facing eastward. His cell mate watched in silence, well aware of what these prayers were all about, having observed Manuel de Lucena do the same while he shared a cell with him.

The next morning, Luis took whatever drinking water was at hand and washed himself from head to foot. Diaz had seen this before, too, when Manuel had performed the same act. He was silent for awhile, then he asked, "Why are you in prison?"

The expression on Luis' face was placid as he said, "I am following God's wishes and commands."

Diaz hesitated. "I see you are a devout man. Is that not enough for God to ask? What wish or command would put you into this jeopardy?"

As anxious as he was to engage in discussion, Luis knew that first he must test the identity of the priest. "I am Luis de Carvajal, *el Mozo*. Perhaps you have heard of me?"

Diaz shook his head in disbelief. "Is it really you? The Lord has blessed me. I have wanted to speak with you ever since I heard of your good works. I am a priest, yes," he lowered his voice to a whisper, "but I am from a family of 'good people'."

Luis could not believe his ears. The term "good people" was used by Secret Jews to identify each other. *What good fortune! Adonai has sent me this man, a son of Secret Jews, so that we may spend our time in mutual prayer and adoration of the Lord*, he thought. Falling to his knees, he cried out, "Blessed is the Lord who answers His servant's needs. Now I can die happily, for I can teach another to love the God of the Law of Moses." He embraced Diaz, who was quick to say that he was anxious to learn everything Luis could teach him.

In the days that followed, encouraged by the intense interest displayed by his companion, Luis explained the significance of many Jewish rituals and procedures. When the priest questioned him about his eating habits, Luis detailed the laws concerning forbidden foods and the reasons for fasting on certain days, as he had done with Friar de Luna previously. He sang his hymns and recited some of his poetry, even telling him about the hiding place of his memoirs and original compositions.

One day, during a discussion, Luis withdrew a copy of the Ten Commandments from the lining of his hat. He explained, "When they brought me here, they confiscated my copies of Psalms, Prophets and Genesis, but they did not find these precious papers."

Diaz looked at the manuscript. "I am most impressed with you, Luis, and am eager to learn all you can teach me."

Early one Sunday morning, a week later, a jailer entered the cell and announced, "Padre Diaz, you are summoned to appear before the Inquisitorial Board immediately."

As he was leaving, Luis called to him. "Padre, I shall pray for you."

When the jailer and his prisoner were down the hall, some distance away from Luis' cell, the priest smiled maliciously and remarked, "He would be wiser to pray for the soul of Luis, *el Mozo*, eh?"

"For sure." The jailer grinned back and nodded.

Luis wondered if Diaz would be released. The padre had mentioned that he hoped to be free soon, that he did not anticipate too much resistance from the inquisitors. "If this should happen," Luis had asked him, "would you be kind enough to retrieve my hidden papers from the ceiling in the prayer room of our house? If you are able to do that, please deliver the papers to my brother-in-law Antonio who lives here in Mexico City. He will see to it that these papers are sent to my brothers in Europe."

Diaz had promised, "I shall certainly do that for you."

Later in the day, as Luis sat alone, he suddenly heard a slight movement outside his door. A piece of paper appeared from under it. He rushed to pick it up. There were only three words scrawled on it: "Diaz Betrayed Manuel."

Luis became feverish. A heavy gloom descended upon him as he speculated, *Who had sent this warning...too late...Oh, God, how could I have been so misled by this fiend?* He spent half the night pleading for a sign from the "most Holy on high". At last, he fell into a restless sleep during which another vision presented itself. He was at a sumptuous banquet in Paradise. The guests were Secret Jews, many of whom he recognized. Those who had been most faithful to the Lord were bedecked with garlands of flowers, joyfully relishing their sweet fragrance and beauty. At the head of the table, he and Justa sat beside the Lord. He awoke with a start. Luis interpreted this dream as a reaffirmation. *I am the Lord's shepherd and will bring the greatest rewards to those Secret Jews who have served Adonai unselfishly. They shall enjoy the closest proximity to Him, a state of bliss. This was God's plan,* Luis was sure. *I must face my inevitable fate and then I shall enjoy the salvation that awaits me. That is more important than life itself.* Even though the hour was late, he made a decision and shouted at the top of his voice, "Jailer, jailer, I want an audience with the High Tribunal. Do you hear me? I demand an audience!"

The sound of departing footsteps echoed loudly down the hallway. No words were needed. He knew their destination.

Surprisingly, he heard nothing about his outburst, but the next evening, Diaz was returned to his cell. The priest greeted him. "Luis, my friend, good to see you again. As you can see, I am still here."

Furious at his deceit, Luis confronted him. "You are a disgrace as a man of the cloth. I am aware of the despicable role you are playing. As for myself, I do not care. I have called for an audience before the court. Right now, I can only hope that, at least, you will have the decency to say nothing about my mother and sisters."

Diaz, surprised and shocked by the revealing declaration, tried to appeal to Luis by denying his accusations, protesting his innocence. Luis would not speak to him.

The following Sunday morning, the jailer again came for Carlos Diaz. Luis waited until their retreating footsteps could no longer be heard before he began shouting, "Beware the priest who is a deceiver and betrayer. Beware the cell mate of Manuel de Lucena and Luis de Carvajal."

He heard the sound of a footfall outside his door and a voice, warning, "Be quiet, de Carvajal, or you shall suffer the rack and the rope again." Unexpectedly, the door was opened with great caution and a figure quickly entered, whispering, "Senor, remember me? Last time — the warden, Alejandro?"

Luis peered at him carefully and recognized the rotund little fellow who had been a well of information — for a price. "Yes, yes, of course. Senor Alejandro —"

The jailer cut him off. "I cannot talk now, but I will have some news soon. I must go." He shut and bolted the door quickly behind him within seconds.

Hope surged within Luis' being. Thank the Lord. *At last, a helping hand.* No one had been to Casa Chata since he was imprisoned and he wondered about his mother and sisters. There had been no clothing, no fruits, no deposit of funds brought to pay for his sequestration. He wondered, *Where were Antonio, Arturo, and the rest of the family?* His food remained untouched as he maintained a twenty-four hour fast and vigil.

The next night, there was another note under the door: 'Family Acapulco Asia' He stared at the message. Tears of joy filled his eyes and he realized the significance of those words. The family had gotten away! *What good fortune — another miracle! Blessed be the Lord who showeth mercy to His servants.*

Several days had passed since the cryptic message under the door. Luis was grateful that Adonai had taken the family "out of bondage." He resolved that he would meet his destiny with strength and courage, knowing that his reward will be with the Lord in salvation.

That Wednesday night, as he lay dozing, he was startled by the sounds of muffled voices and sobbing coming from the corridor. A woman was asking loudly, "My son, where are you?" Luis felt as if a dagger had pierced his heart. He recognized his mother's voice. Someone silenced her but Luis managed to yell, "I hear you, Mother. The Lord give you strength." A gruff voice admonished him to "shut his mouth." To add to the pain Luis felt, the next sounds confirmed that his sisters were there as well.

His depression was indescribable. Heavy of heart, he asked of Adonai, "Why are they lost? Why? Why have You taken them to such heights of expectation only to bring them down to this utter despair? I beg for Your divine guidance." Hours later, when he heard the jailers making their rounds, he realized it must be morning. His mind raced to muster every bit of intelligence he possessed; he must devise a scheme. Soon he would be called to the "devils' hall," perhaps to be charged.

On February 9, 1595, at eight o'clock in the morning, two guards entered his cell. They escorted him to the Hall of the Inquisition where, much to his distress, he was brought before his nemesis, Licentiate Alonso de Peralta. Also present were Inquisitor Lobo Guerrero and Dr. Martos de Bohorques, the prosecuting attorney for the Holy Office. Inquisitor Guerrero looked at the young man before him and experienced the same sensation he had felt when he interrogated Luis in the past. He had recognized even then that this was no ordinary man. Luis was a zealot, one with great determination and intense faith. The inquisitor could not help but admire him.

The clerk brought Luis forward and swore him in, then Peralta presented the charges against him: "On this ninth day of February, in the year of our Lord, 1595, you, Luis de Carvajal, el Mozo, have been summoned before this High Tribunal of the Holy Office of Mexico City to face charges of crimes against the Catholic Church. Witnesses have given evidence that you are a '*Judaizante relapso pertinaz*', that you have reverted to your old practice of worshipping the Dead Law of Moses and that you have instructed others to follow in this belief. How do you answer?"

"I deny the charges. They are not true, sir. I was reconciled in the auto-da-fe of 1590, as were other members of my family, and we have lived as faithful Catholics, ever abiding by the Evangelical Law of Grace of Jesus Christ, our Redeemer."

The inquisitor continued. "The Court is well aware of your history. You and your family were taken back into the bosom of Mother Church, in good faith. You, Luis, as well as your mother and sisters, abjured 'de vehementi', wherein you all swore never to relapse to the Old Religion, under penalty of death by the bonfire. Information received by this Holy Office indicates that you all have acted contrary to your vows."

Luis fell to his knees and proclaimed their innocence. "We have been wrongly accused. You must believe me. We are good Christians."

As was his custom, Peralta suddenly stood up and instructed the warden to take the prisoner back to his cell. He suggested to Luis, "Perhaps some additional deliberation will refresh your memory. Maybe next time, you will have more to offer...maybe even some information about your friends."

The statement made Luis shudder. They were not going to be content with just the heads of the de Carvajals.

Luis' assessment was correct. During the next few weeks, he was taken to the torture chamber five times and, each time, he was subjected to the ropes. The jailer tied his arms together loosely behind his back and every time Luis gave an unsatisfactory answer, the inquisitor ordered that the ropes be twisted and tightened. The warden and clergy in attendance urged Luis to "tell the truth." He held fast to his denials until, at last, fainting from the pain and suffering endless hours of unbearable punishment, he cried out, "I confess. I did return to the Law of Moses. I alone did this. My family continued in their devotion to the Lord Jesus Christ —"

Guerrero interrupted, "Luis, why do you persist in this lie?"

"Sirs, I beseech you," Luis pleaded. "The truth is that I, and I alone, am the only *'relapso'*. The others are faithful to the cross."

Peralta ordered another twist of the ropes.

Almost fainting again, the prisoner began to mumble names of those with whom he had Judaized, names of people he knew were no longer in the area, or deceased. It was an essential deception. He needed a reprieve from the agony.

Ordering the jailer to cease the punishment, Peralta advised Luis that he would see him again soon and added menacingly, "In the interim, it would be wise to refresh your recollections a little further so that, next time, your information may save you from a revisit to the 'confessional'."

Two days later, he was again summoned before an angry Peralta. "Perhaps today you will tell us about your friends — those that are still alive and in Mexico City. You had better not try anymore tricks, liar."

So, they had checked the names, Luis mused.

"What can you tell us today?" Peralta glared at him.

"Nothing. I have nothing to say." Luis' eyes narrowed in defiance and his jaw set like steel tempered by fire.

This infuriated Peralta. "Take him to the torture chamber and strip him down."

After suffering terribly on the ropes, Luis began a litany of names which included his family, close friends, and anybody else he could think of. Injured physically and emotionally, he submitted to the torture. Satisfied with the results of their "holy work", the inquisitors ordered Luis back to his cell, but not before saying, "You have done well, my boy."

As they half-dragged, half-carried him down the hallway, the remorse and anger Luis felt overwhelmed him. In desperation, with every ounce of strength left, he broke away from his captors as they were passing an open stairway and flung himself down the steep, stone steps to the courtyard. Luis wished to die.

Considering the fall, the injuries proved to be minor. His arm was broken and his left leg, badly sprained. He found it ironic, in days to come, that they cared for his injuries until he was sufficiently healed, inasmuch as they were killing him, little by little, in the torture chamber.

Adequately recovered, he was again summoned before the High Tribunal within a couple of weeks. The inquisitors pressed for specific and conclusive evidence against those whom Luis had named. The amanuensis stood ready to record his testimony and to witness his signature on the documents of incrimination. Peralta could barely conceal his glee at this triumph. It was short-lived.

All of a sudden, after he was sworn in, Luis stated, "I wish to recant my entire testimony which was given under the duress of extreme torture. The only reason I mentioned all those names was to save myself from further suffering. It was all lies — lies from the start of my torment to the end. I have borne false witness against the people I have named."

The inquisitors and the others present were astounded by the prisoner's unexpected retraction. Guerrero asked, "Luis, did you not have enough of the ropes? Why are you recanting? Why are you lying now?"

"No, now I do not lie. This is the truth. Demons plagued me and made me act falsely. But I have dealt with my conscience and I would rather suffer earthly pain than go to hell for testifying dishonestly."

Guerrero continued, "Why this sudden change of heart? You are not thinking clearly; you are foolish to do this."

"No, I was foolish to think only of myself and place others in jeopardy with untruths. I have had a revelation, a vision that has shown me the way."

"And which way is that?" a snarling Peralta demanded.

"The way that the God of the Law of Moses has shown me. Even though I lived my life in such a manner that others believed I had converted to the Evangelical Law, I have never faltered in my belief that the Mosaic Law is the true faith. Adonai is the Lord and only through Him will I find salvation."

Peralta's face contorted with frustration. He bellowed for the guard. "Remove the heretic!" Then with a withering look at Luis, he said scathingly, "Go back to Casa Chata and wait for your salvation. Let us see what your God will do for you now. Your soul is damned, de Carvajal. Nothing can save you."

Viper, Luis thought, *my body shall suffer at your hands but you will never touch my soul. Adonai will prepare a seat for me at his table.*

CHAPTER XXIII

HOPE SPRINGS ETERNAL

After almost a week of deep thought and prayer, Antonio decided that he would send Arturo to Casa Chata again, to seek out their 'cooperates-for-dinero' warden. Luckily, when Arturo arrived at the jail, Alejandro was still on duty. The jailer whispered that he had delivered the message from Senor de Caceres to Senor de Carvajal.

"I will leave this package of linens for Luis and some gifts for the senoras. You will see to it that they get them, *por favor.*" There was a surreptitious shift of money and a mutual nod. "I shall return within a few days," Arturo advised him. "Please try to have some news for me."

"For sure, Senor — Friday, at midday," Alejandro assured him with a conspiratorial wink. "Gracias."

The days seemed endless. On Friday, Antonio waited for Arturo to return from Casa Chata. As soon as his cousin came through the door, he immediately sensed something was wrong. His cousin recounted what the warden had told him of Luis' torture and of the implication of the family and friends. "And then," Arturo continued, "when Luis was brought before the High Tribunal again, he recanted everything. He swore it was a pack of lies, dragged from his lips by excessive torture and that he alone is the only Judaizer in his family. Needless to say, the inquisitors were furious. Antonio, I am afraid his doom is certain and Francisca and the girls are in the same dire circumstances."

Antonio stood silent as a pillar of stone, absorbing the details, his heart heavy with sorrow. In a resolute voice, he told Arturo, "I shall ask for an audience before the Holy Office. My reputation as a good Christian has never been in question. I will promise them anything, including a good deal of what I own. That should melt their hard hearts. Do not speak any further with the warden. Let us see what I can accomplish."

After Arturo left, Antonio sat late into the night checking his papers and tallying the figures representing his financial status. He sifted through the deeds to lands and ownership certificates to mines, trying to decide just what he might be forced to relinquish. *To save the family,* he swore, *he would give the devils his entire estate.*

The next morning, Antonio presented himself at the Office of the Inquisition and requested an audience with Inquisitors Peralta and Guerrero. The clerk told him to be seated in the waiting room while he checked to see if they were available. After forty-five minutes, Antonio was invited into a large chamber at the end of the hallway. The room was lavishly decorated with valuable paintings and expensive oriental rugs. He could not help thinking, *I wonder whose confiscated property paid for all this abundance?* A gorgeous teakwood desk, gold-leafed with a delicate design, stood in the middle of the room. *Nothing but the best for these scoundrels, eh?* His mental meandering came to an abrupt halt at the sound of a loud, officious voice.

"What did you wish to see us about, Senor de Caceres? A license for a ship perhaps, or do you wish to sell us some lovely items you have brought back from other lands?" Peralta, smug and condescending, with a smile that did not reach his eyes, had asked the question.

Antonio knew he was being badgered. *I would like to smash your silly face,* he thought, but instead he smiled solicitously. This was no time to lose his temper. "Sirs, you know me and that I live my life as a Christian and conduct my household in a Christian manner, according to the law of Jesus Christ, our Savior. I was never aware of any member of my family relapsing into the Old Religion. If any did, then evil spirits must have influenced them. I know, with proper guidance, they can be reconciled with the Church. I beg of you to forego the protocol of extreme punishment for 'relapsos pertinaz'."

Peralta interrupted, "You are a knowledgeable man, de Caceres. You know that we must deal with these 'relapsos' as proscribed by law. At the last trial of the de Carvajals, when they were reconciled with the Church, they took an oath, in writing, pledging eternal allegiance to the Pope and the Catholic Church. This they have failed to do."

"Sirs, I beg of you," Antonio pleaded, "I appeal to your generosity and goodness of heart to reconsider. My wife Catalina has brought up our daughter Leonor as child of the Catholic faith. We will continue to live our lives in that faith, I promise you. People make mistakes and sometimes stray from the path of righteousness. Who knows what devils made them their prey? But I swear to you, I shall personally take the responsibility of keeping my family in the true faith."

The inquisitors sat quietly for several minutes. Then Peralta asked, "Would you be willing to sign a statement to that effect and suffer the penalties if you are not successful?"

"Yes, yes, anything. I will sign anything." Antonio felt encouraged.

Guerrero leaned over to Peralta and whispered in his ear. Peralta nodded. "Senor de Caceres," he turned to Antonio, "come back in three days and we shall have a decision for you. Good day."

Antonio started to say something but both inquisitors disappeared through a side door before the first syllable escaped his lips. Well, at least, he was thankful, they had not said no.

The next three days were unbearable. Antonio paced up and down, frustrated and sick at heart. Only the children could put a smile upon his face. For the next two nights, after the girls went to sleep, he stayed awake for hours, praying that he will be able to save the family. It was finally the third day. Antonio went back to the Holy Office, where he again waited and, again, was shown into the elegant chamber of his previous interview. The stern-faced inquisitors entered, took seats behind the exquisite desk and faced their visitor.

Peralta spoke first. "Senor de Caceres, we have no hope to offer you. Your brother-in-law, Luis de Carvajal, *el Mozo*, has expressed his desire and willingness to die for the God of the Law of Moses. Soon, his mother and sisters will be required to give testimony. Eventually, they will all be remanded to the secular authority for sentencing."

A shocked Antonio decided that it was time for his final ploy. "Sirs, I am prepared to offer you a large sum of money and valuable land wherein I own many silver mines, if you will reconsider."

He described the properties and the inquisitors were impressed — and tempted — but Alonso de Peralta was looking beyond the horizon. He had already formulated ideas for an impressive auto-da-fe, a grand one that would bring him into the prominence and prestige that would certainly elevate him to the office of bishop. Nothing now would alter that plan.

"Senor de Caceres, this interview is at an end. There is no more to be said other than we urge you to go home and continue living as a good Christian."

Downcast and desperate, Antonio took his leave. He thought, *If ever there was a time for a miracle, it was now.*

The two inquisitors could not help but think about the wealth that had been offered them. "Let us make a note of this, for future reference," Peralta suggested. "Interesting information, I must say — and not to be forgotten."

Guerrero replied, "I agree."

Antonio could hear the crying even before he entered the house. Sweating profusely, he flung open the door. Emilia and Leonor were huddled at the foot of the stairs, hysterical. "They have arrested Anica!" the nanny cried out.

"What? Who did this?" He knew the answer even before he asked. "The miserable curs! While I was pleading for the lives of our loved ones, the underhanded cowards came to my home, behind my back, and took Luis' little sister. How much blood do these vampires need? Poor, sick little one...Anica...Oh, Lord, is she not suffering enough?" Antonio was in a rage, cursing the Holy Office and swearing his revenge.

"Please, sir, control yourself or we shall all surely be arrested," Emilia pleaded.

"You are right. Temper will get me nowhere," he said slowly, his voice a monotone, devoid of any hope.

His daughter pulled at his arm. "Daddy, what will happen to Anica? Can we go to see her? What shall we tell Grandma?"

"Leonor, my darling one, so many questions at once —" The innocence of children! How could he tell his daughter that her mother, grandmother and aunts were all in jail? Holding her close, he kissed the top of her head and cajoled, "Come, little one, we shall go for a walk and I will buy you your favorite chocolates. Would you like that?"

With a quick sweep of her little hand, she wiped away a tear that had lingered on her bottom lash. "Yes, Papa." She stifled a sob and flashed her father a brave but fleeting smile.

Antonio decided that the wisest way to proceed was to maintain a low profile. If the Inquisition decided to pounce upon him, who would be left on the outside to help? His cousin was a willing go-between, but he had neither the resources nor the connections to be of much assistance. As he sat there deliberating, a scheme began to formulate in his mind. But could it be accomplished?

Knowing how corrupt most of the jailers were, money being the greatest motivation for disloyalty, he determined to make Alejandro an offer he would find difficult to resist. He would send Arturo to Casa Chata with a bag of fruit for little Anica and also with a proposal for the warden Alejandro.

When Arturo arrived at the jail, the warden was nowhere in sight; another one was on duty. There had been a change in shifts apparently. He dared not ask; instead, he told the jailer to see to it that the little girl received the fruit.

The next afternoon he returned to the jail at a later hour, at four o'clock, hoping to find Alejandro on duty. He brought some items of clothing with him that he would say he had forgotten to bring the day before, if an excuse were needed. This time, luckily, Alejandro was on duty in the front vestibule. No one else was present. Inside the jail, the food trays were being distributed to the inmates and Alejandro took advantage of the moment to say, in his customary whisper, "Senor, the sister Mariana has been sent to the Hospital for Invalids. The poor woman seems to have gone mad. And the little one, Anica — she is being questioned by the inquisitors. The rest of the family are suffering on the rack and that is enough to wring a confession from a stone." He looked knowingly at Arturo. "You understand?"

Arturo nodded. The warden was telling him that the probability of confession by the women in the torture chamber was imminent. He compensated his informant and hinted about needing his help, for a price, in the near future. The jailer's response was most encouraging. As they shook hands, Arturo slipped him a note for Luis.

Antonio sat staring into space. Arturo had just told him of the latest developments. Abruptly, he asked his cousin, "Do you have confidence in this warden Alejandro?" and without waiting for a response, he added, "I have a plan for the family's escape."

Eyebrows raised in amazement, Arturo said nothing and waited to hear more.

"Would it be possible to get from this jailer a night schedule of the wardens at the jail and also a drawing showing where the exits are to the courtyard in back of Casa Chata? What do you think? Can we trust this man?"

Scratching his head and rubbing the stubbly growth on his chin, Arturo responded slowly, "How can anyone be sure these days, but I think our friend could be convinced to help if you would guarantee his freedom from financial worry — like an early retirement. He has mentioned several times how he hates working in that 'hellhole'."

"Good. If he helps us, I shall see to it that he enjoys bright, sunny days as a man of leisure for many years to come. Now listen carefully. This is what I want you to do. First, you must approach our robust friend and settle things with him. If he agrees, then we must decide on a night when he is on duty and in charge of securing the cells and outside doors. Guillermo, Emilia's brother, has confirmed that Francisca and Isabel are together in one cell;

Catalina and Anica, in another; Leonor, alone, next to them; and, Luis, down the hallway, near the torture chamber. All are in the same corridor, luckily.

"Their doors must be left unlocked and the exit doors unbolted that night. The family needs to be alerted to the details of the escape so that they will be ready to leave at a given signal. You and Nazareo will be in the wooded area behind the courtyard, waiting in a covered wagon, to take them away to safety."

"Where can we take them, Antonio?" the cousin asked.

"I will handle those details. You will drive to Taxco where you will stay overnight and, in the morning, change horses and head for Tlatlelco. Friends in both places will assist you according to my instructions. I will give you more information when I have finalized the arrangements. Now we must determine if our discontented warden is ready to make a commitment. Let us wait a few days to approach him. Meanwhile, I shall ride to Taxco and Tlatelco to secure assistance and safe haven for all of you."

"What will we tell Francisca about Mariana? Perhaps she already knows?" Arturo asked.

"She may. Anyway, Mariana is ill and is better off in hospital for the time being. We can do nothing about it now." Antonio shook his head.

"What about you and little Leonor?"

"I will follow with my daughter and Emilia a little while after you leave the prison with the family and will meet up with you eventually in Tlatlelco. Let us hope we can hide there and be able to make further plans." Antonio embraced his cousin. "*Vaya con Dios.*"

In the week that followed, every facet of the escape plan fell into place. With Alejandro's promised cooperation, it could not fail. Luis and the women were alerted and told to wait for three soft taps on their doors, sometime after midnight, on Friday. The warden would direct them to the open door to the courtyard.

At last it was Friday night and the de Carvajals could barely contain their excitement. They sat in their cells, clutching their few meager belongings, waiting for the miracle.

Well after midnight, Arturo and Nazareo sat in their wagon, anticipating passengers at any moment. Suddenly, they heard a great commotion and saw soldiers with torches running all over the courtyard. Apprehensive, they stayed in the shadows, watching. If the men were to get any closer to the perimeter of the jail grounds, they would surely see the wagon. They dared not move. All of a sudden, someone shouted an order from the building and the soldiers ran back.

It was bedlam in Casa Chata. Two wardens were running up and down the corridors, checking cell doors, noting which ones were unlocked. By now, all the prisoners were awake and in a state of anxiety, yelling, asking questions. Once quiet was restored, Inquisitors Peralta and Guerrero appeared. They approached Luis' cell, calling out his name.

Luis was in a state of collapse. All hopes for the rescue attempt were shattered. He wondered how these accursed inquisitors had found out. His cell door opened and by the flickering light of a torch, he could make out two black-robed figures whom he recognized immediately.

"Where is your God tonight, Luis?" the familiar voice of his nemesis asked. Peralta and Guerrero chuckled and slammed the door shut behind them, not waiting for an answer.

"My Lord is waiting for me to take my seat beside Him," Luis whispered to the darkness. "It is God's will."

Warden Alejandro reflected on the bad luck. All had been going according to plan. He had unlocked the cell doors and left the exit gate unbolted. In a few minutes, he would have signaled the de Carvajals and led them out...The jailer drew a deep breath. One can never anticipate the unexpected. Who would have thought that one of the other jailers would have reported for his shift earlier than usual?

"You are not on duty for another hour, my friend," Alejandro had reminded him.

"Yes, I know. I had a disagreement with my wife, so I left the house to let her cool off. It is much more pleasant here." The jailer laughed raucously.

"Why do you not go home, try to patch it up? A little squeeze, a kiss..."Alejandro had winked broadly and poked the jailer in the ribs with his elbow. "A little monkey business, eh, and all will be forgiven."

"You do not know my wife. She will break me like a twig. No, I do not go back tonight." Saying that, he had looked long and hard into Alejandro's face — enough to arouse a feeling of discomfort in the conspirator. At that instance, Alejandro had made a judicious decision and one not too soon for two soldiers were dismounting in front of the jail.

"I shall return in a minute. I need to urinate," he had informed his colleague and promptly disappeared down the hall. As he hastened away, he thought, *Someone has gotten wind of the scheme, no doubt.* "Damn," he cursed aloud. Exiting the building, he cautiously stayed in the shadows until he reached his horse. He could hear the raised voices inside as he mounted and eased his steed toward the woods. There was nothing more he could do except to get as far away as possible. Lovingly patting his saddlebag, filled with Antonio's generous 'gift', he looked back only once. "God be with you," he murmured and made the sign of the cross.

Only Arturo and Nazareo noticed a rider taking off at a rapid pace into the darkness.

CHAPTER XXIV

RESOLVE

After the disaster of the foiled rescue attempt, Luis knew that more than ever his loved ones needed uplifting. He sent messages on banana peels and scratched signs and words on the shells of nuts or eggs and on pieces of fruit. Such contacts were accomplished only with the help of the jailers who, in turn, were reporting everything to the Holy Office. When the inquisitors heard of this "correspondence", they instructed the jailers to leave paper, pen and an inkwell in Luis' cell. What they were hoping for was that Luis, in letters to his family, would involve them and betray other Judaizers. This never happened.

Luis took advantage of this "miracle of the paper" to write loving, inspired messages to his mother and sisters, encouraging them to be brave and maintain their faith in Adonai. In moving passages, he described how the Lord will open the Gates of Righteousness and let them into Paradise where heavenly bliss awaited them.

To Isabel and Leonor, he wrote: "Oh, flock of my soul, so scattered are you! Cheer up, cheer up, says the Lord, for I shall free them from the wolves and put them in sweet pastures...I wish I could see you and greet you for a while. I beg God to grant me my wish of seeing you, but if not, I am comforted by the thought that we shall see each other before death, and afterward for an eternity in the land of glory, among the beautiful angels and saints...."

Luis was careful in all his letters to insist that he alone was guilty. Everything else he said vindicated the family. To his sister Catalina, he wrote, "God's blessed gift of my life, may the sweet God visit you and comfort you. Through a miracle of His, I received some ink so that I can write to you. Although I pretend otherwise in front of you all, the truth is that my heart never parted from the law of God. So I have confessed and do confess concerning myself alone, because to say otherwise would be to give false testimony. You are going, as Queen Sheba did, to visit the beautiful and wise King of Angels, to see His rich palaces and gardens and paradise, and to eat His sweet foods...You will be bathed in perfumed waters...We shall dance and sing with Him....How the blessed Father, whom you awaited and believed in, will embrace you!"

When Luis learned of the arrest of his youngest sister Anica, it destroyed every last vestige of hope. *Even a child*, he thought. *These demons knew no bounds*. Writing to Anica was difficult for him. Her illness had caused her much pain but he was always able to keep her spirits up through prayer and the faith in a better time to come. In one of his letters, he told her, "Ana dear, my blessed one, apple of my eye, and soul of my heart. May the strong God and Lord visit you and strengthen you...Rejoice and be happy, blessed daughter, that this is the road to paradise and to the glory that awaits...Oh, what beautiful necklaces of pearl and opal the Lord will order to be placed on your injured neck, my martyr; oh, what beautiful chains of gold and what jewels in return for all that you have suffered...what beauties He will show you, what paradises, what orchards and gardens...what streams of milk and honey! May He visit you and save you, amen. I am the Almighty's slave, though unworthy."

In letters to his sisters, Luis was strong but his inner despair showed when he wrote to his mother, "O, mother of my soul, the Spirit of God be with you...Oh, mother of my heart, may the holy Lord see your affliction and guard you and assuage you. May he cover you and your children with His holy blessing...may God free you from prison, and sin, and jail, and hell, amen, amen, amen, amen..."

May of 1595 brought more grief. Justa and her mother were arrested. While they were being taken to their cells, Luis recognized who they were, not only by Justa's sweet, familiar voice, but the remarks she made. Loudly, she proclaimed, "I am innocent of any crime. My mother and I are good Christians!"

Luis, amidst all his misery, heard the words of his beloved. Sadly, he shook his head and a look of desolation crossed his face. *Brave Justa, my sweet love*, he thought. *She was making sure that I know she is in Casa Chata*. In his next letter to Leonor, he asked if she knew what cell Justa and Clara occupied. He wished to write to her but he decided that he dared not, in spite of how much he longed to. "Dear Lord," he entreated, "give Justa guidance and forgive her for feigning to be a 'good Christian'."

There were many letters during the spring and summer of that year — and all of them were shown to the inquisitors, to whose frustration, not one letter incriminated anyone but Luis. The Holy Office had not outwitted Luis who was too clever to credit the inkwell, pen, and paper totally to a miracle.

He had surmised that even though the jailers seemed anxious to deliver messages amongst the family members, there was a real possibility that the inquisitors were being apprised of every word he wrote. If the inquisitors had any hopes that Luis would mention the names of other Judaizers, those hopes were shattered as time passed and they recognized the futility of trying to entrap him.

Peralta and Guerrero held several meetings to discuss how they should proceed with the case against Luis. They decided to summon two theologians to debate with the prisoner in the hope that they would convert him. When they advised Luis that he will be visited by two priests, he answered, "I look forward to it. If they can convince me, I shall convert because more than anything else, I wish to save my soul from eternal damnation." Actually, Luis was considering a different potential. Perhaps he could convince them that the God of the Law of Moses is the only true God.

Pedro de Agurto and Diego de Contreras, both learned Augustinians, spent five evenings with Luis. They were impressed with his extreme religiosity and sincerity and the conviction with which he spoke. At one point, Luis was asked by Father de Agurto, "Do you believe in the hereafter?"

"Most certainly." Luis responded with a quote from Deuteronomy. "God said, 'My children, everything that I created in the Universe is in pairs, for example, heaven and earth, sun and moon, Adam and Eve, this world and the world to come — but I am one and alone in the Universe'."

"Do you deny the doctrine of the Holy Trinity and Mary, the mother of Jesus Christ?"

"Yes," answered Luis, "because in Exodus, God declares, 'I am the first, for I have no father, and I am the last for I have no brother, and besides me, there is no God, for I have no son'."

The theologians exchanged glances, shrugged and told Luis, "We shall return another evening. The Lord Jesus Christ be with you and lead you into the path of the righteous." Padre Contreras made the sign of the cross and both priests withdrew from the cell.

During their next four visits, the priests again debated the concept of Jesus as the son of God. Luis was adamant. At one point, he quoted a fourth-century rabbi: "Strange are those men who believe that God had a son and suffered him to die....Would He have looked on calmly while His son was being slain and not have reduced the world to chaos?"

Father Agurto responded, "Matthew 3:17: And lo a voice from heaven... This is my beloved son, in whom I am well pleased."

Luis countered with, "I am one and alone in the Universe, saith the Lord God."

"Are you not afraid of the sentence which awaits you for this heresy?" asked Father Contreras.

"No, I am not. Even your Jesus said, 'Blessed are they which are persecuted for righteousness' sake for theirs is the kingdom of heaven'."

"But," rebutted the priest, "unless you accept the Lord Jesus Christ, you will be denied heaven."

Luis answered, "Not so. Adonai has promised salvation to those who keep the covenant and follow His Law."

"That Law, the Law of Moses, is dead," Father Agurto replied.

Luis asked, "Do you not preach, observe and believe in the Ten Commandments? Did not your Evangelical Law come from the Law that God handed down to Moses?"

"Yes," answered Father Agurto, "but that Law has been changed and improved and the Old Law is dead."

"Changed? How so?" Luis stated, "In Matthew 5:18, did not Jesus say, '...till heaven and earth pass, one jot or one tittle shall in no wise pass from the law, till all be fulfilled'?"

The priests continued to be amazed at Luis' knowledge of chapter and verse, and thus it continued, two seasoned prelates and a young zealot, each professing what he believed to be the truth, each holding fast to that belief. By the end of the fifth session, it was obvious to the theologians that Luis could not be swayed. They bade him goodbye and bestowed a blessing upon him, "The grace of our Lord Jesus Christ be with you, Luis."

He responded with, "Isaiah 41: Fear not for I will strengthen thee, for I the Lord thy God will hold thy right hand. I am the Lord your Holy One, the creator of Israel, your King."

The priests closed the cell door, their hearts heavy with a sadness that they could not deny. Peralta and Guerrero will find no satisfaction in their news.

During those summer months, Luis' mother and sisters were subjected to torture. At one point, during her suffering, Francisca cried out, "*Miserere mei!* Have mercy upon me," and the pain being inflicted was so unbearable that she confessed to Judaizing with her children and close friends.

Her daughters did not fair any better and the confessions flowed. Isabel, who had been so beautiful and vibrant, was subjected to such agony that she could barely stand on her feet. An amanuensis was summoned to her cell and she confirmed the secret observances of her family. Her physical condition was so depleted that she could not even sign her depositions. Yet the inquisitors persisted in their questioning.

"I have told you everything," she insisted tearfully. "I only wish to say that my little sister Anica is innocent of any participation in clandestine practices. I beg you to consider that. She is only a child and does not comprehend."

"It will be so noted in the record." The secretary asked for her oral confirmation of what he had written. She listened as he read his notes and she attested to them.

As his family's suffering continued, so did Luis'. Peralta, adamant in his desire to convert him, paid him several visits in his cell. These meetings proved to be unproductive and, in fact, were a source of irritation. Finally, Luis told him, "I am preparing my last will and testament that I shall sign as Joseph Lumbroso. I have nothing further to say."

Peralta stared at him for a moment, seething and frustrated, and then, without a word, exited.

During the harrowing months that followed, smuggled messages kept coming from Antonio. Even though he tried to encourage them by telling them how hard he was working toward their release, he and they knew that time was growing short and hope was rapidly diminishing. Then one unhappy day, Guillermo slipped a message from Emilia to Luis telling him that Antonio had been arrested and his little girl placed with a Catholic family.

One evening, when Guillermo was depositing the food tray inside the cell, Luis whispered, "Have you seen Justa Mendez?"

"Yes," he answered quickly and left at once, fearful of being overheard by the jailer who was approaching.

Luis would have asked more but he understood the danger in which he placed his friend. He decided to have a letter ready for Justa next time. With heavy heart, he sat on his crude bench and wrote, "My darling Justa, My loving thoughts are with you always. I pray for you and your dear mother.

May Adonai be with you and deliver you from this wicked captivity. I wish you were by my side, sharing a life together in service and devotion to the glory of God. My dearest, we are but the dust of stars, solitary sprinklings in the loneliness of night. May the Lord bless you ever and ever. With love, Luis."

The next morning, awaking with a start at the sound of metal scraping the stone floor, Luis glimpsed Guillermo's face as he projected a meaningful glance towards the food tray. Luis quickly handed him the note he had written to Justa. Guillermo left without a word. Luis bent down to pick up the tray. There was a note tucked under a bowl. Eagerly he tore it open. Tears filled his eyes as he read: "My beloved Luis, Love of my life and my soul. My prayers and hopes are dedicated to your well being and safety. I beseech the Lord to keep you in His care through these terrible days. You are always in my heart and thoughts and when I lie down to sleep, you are by my side. Your devoted Justa."

Luis held the note in his hands, tenderly caressing the words with his fingers and pressing the page to his cheek and to his lips. He read it again and again and wept. As he wept, he begged, "Lord of the Universe, take pity on this sinner for his weakness. How I long to hold her in my arms just once again." Overcome with guilt, he whispered to the foul, heavy air in his dungeon, "May the good Lord forgive me for my transgressions."

Sleep was the enemy. In between fitful moments of restlessness and slumber, visions of Justa and Heaven transposed themselves intermittently. He saw himself running, first to Justa and then to God, both of whom stood with arms outstretched to him. This vision, Luis believed, was divine guidance. He must not allow himself to stray, even in thought, from the path to glory.

CHAPTER XXV

IN EXTREMO

It was early 1596 before the inquisitors summoned Luis, who was spending most of the time writing letters to his loved ones and completing his Last Will and Testament. From time to time, he was visited by monks and priests whom he engaged in lively discussions. The Holy Office was anxious to effect Luis' conversion because of the impact it would have on the crypto-Jewish community, not to mention the victory for the Church. Peralta, especially, desperately hungered for this triumph; it would be an asset to his personal agenda.

On the morning of February 8th, Luis was informed that he was to appear at a hearing that afternoon. There had been little news about his mother and sisters. Ever so often, he would receive a message or some sign that they, too, were still waiting. He wondered if he would learn anything of their fate this day. Whatever happened, he was determined to remain firm in his denial of their guilt and insist the accusations were true only of him.

When Luis was brought before the Court, he was asked if he had any further information to impart to the Holy Office.

Luis looked at the arrogant and imperious Peralta and replied in a firm and confident tone, "I have told you all I know. I have nothing more to say."

"In that case, Luis de Carvajal, *el Mozo*, you will be tortured '*in extremus*' unless you decide to speak the truth now."

"I have nothing further to disclose." Luis dropped to his knees suddenly and cried out, "O God, give me the strength not to tell lies!"

He was taken away to the "chamber of hell", as Luis referred to it, and within minutes the black-hooded minister was summoned to apply the torture to his victim who lay half-naked on the rack. In between the tightening of the ropes, Luis shouted out some names, at which point the amanuensis recorded them. This procedure continued for three days at the end of which the inquisitors were still not satisfied. They admonished him to consider carefully during the coming weekend what more he can tell them.

On Monday, after a harrowing two days of trying to overcome the pain of the torture, Luis was sent for. This time, he was taken directly to the torture chamber. The intention was to lose no time should he prove uncooperative.

"Well, Luis, are you ready to tell us more about your Secret Jews and their rites and practices?" asked Guerrero.

His answer amazed them. "I have begged the Court not to compel me to tell falsehoods and yet that is exactly what has happened. Extreme torture forced me to lie about everybody I have named. It is all lies and I did this because of your inhuman treatment in this chamber. I and I alone am the only Judaizer."

Fuming, Peralta snarled, "Another recantation? You leave us no choice. I see that more severe methods must be employed to convince you." He gave the signal for Luis to be placed upon the 'potro' — a wooden bed frame — and for the water torture to begin. The warden placed a piece of cheese cloth over Luis' mouth and gradually poured water through it down his throat, the effect of which caused Luis to feel slowly suffocated. Several jars of water were dispensed until finally Luis frantically signaled with his hand. As soon as they removed the cloth, he shouted, "Why not kill me now, for I have nothing more to say."

At this outburst, Guerrero pulled Peralta aside. "Let us meet with Bohorques, the prosecuting attorney, and give him instructions to prepare the case against Luis. He will present his findings to the Court and we will go to trial with our evidence. There is nothing more to be done here."

"Perhaps you are right. I will call Bohorques in the morning. He is my cousin, you know." A sly grin played around the corners of Peralta's mouth.

Luis, broken in spirit and body and totally demoralized, could still hear Peralta's parting advice ringing in his ears: "If you wish salvation and redemption for your evil practices, you would be wise to give up your blind ways and accept the Lord Jesus Christ who, in His gracious goodness, will redeem you and give you everlasting life."

To this, Luis had retorted, loudly, "Only my Lord God of the Universe can do that for me."

The warden had cuffed him hard on the side of the head as he led him away.

On September 12th, 1596, Luis submitted the "Last Will and Testament of Joseph Lumbroso (Luis de Carvajal, *el Mozo*)" to the Inquisitional Court, in which he expressed his thoughts and his desire "to live and die for the holy and true law...and His holy Commandments....I shall joyfully give away my soul for the faith of the Holy Testament...and for His holy truths...in the canticle He taught to Moses."

After reading the document, the inquisitors agreed that it was time for the prosecuting attorney to present the indictment against Luis to the High Tribunal. Peralta himself wrote a blistering condemnation of the prisoner, a fifteen-page tirade on "the heresy and apostasy of Luis de Carvajal who has stated that he wishes to die." He attached these pages to the Last Will and Testament and submitted them, along with the indictment prepared by Bohorques. At the bottom of the will, Peralta had written: "Testament of Joseph Lumbroso (Luis de Carvajal, *el Mozo*) and the final answer he gives, thus definitely concluding his case."

By the end of October, Luis stood before the Court which was comprised of two inquisitors, the prosecuting attorney, and a panel of three priests. He was sworn in and then the clerk began the questioning. He held up a little black leather-bound book and asked, "Do you recognize this?" The book was Luis' in which he had written his memoirs.

"Yes, I do. I wrote in it the details of my life and of the miracles that God in His mercy performed for me."

Peralta interjected angrily, "Why is it that you also wrote of your mother's and sisters' clandestine religious practices which you so vehemently continue to deny?" His voice was like thunder.

The sight of the book stunned Luis momentarily and then he thought, *That sniveling traitor Diaz! He told them where my papers were hidden and they had confiscated the book and, no doubt, some of my poems and hymns.* Luis was slow in answering. All he could think of was that he had to protect his beloved mother and sisters. "I am confused. If I said anything to that effect, then it was only to impress my brothers for whom the book was intended. I wanted them to remember the family in a way that would comfort them inasmuch as they are Jews now living in a free land." Saying these words gave Luis satisfaction that was immediately followed by a feeling of defeat. By his own hand, he had condemned those he loved.

Peralta's next words confirmed this. "Your mother and sisters have already been sentenced. You have lost your battle, Luis."

Hearing those words created such a deep feeling of revulsion that he had to exert tremendous control not to be sick to his stomach, not to cry out in anguish, not to collapse under the weight of this terrible news.

The clerk continued, "Who is it you speak of, in your memoirs, as fleeing on horseback from a commissary of the Inquisition?"

"That is my brother-in-law, Jorge de Almeida."

"Where is this man now?"

"To the best of my knowledge, not in the colonial territories." Luis was evasive.

"Did he not travel to Spain after your first arrest in 1589, and make contacts to secure the release of your mother, sisters, and yourself?"

"Yes, he did."

"Is he a believer in the Dead Law?"

"My brother-in-law has always followed your Evangelical Law." Luis wondered, *Why the resurgence of interest in Jorge?*

"Then why did he choose to disobey the orders of the Inquisition when he returned to Mexico City in 1591?"

"He told me he was concerned that you would arrest him in order to appropriate his wife's estate because you had incarcerated her."

There followed several more questions about Jorge, but Luis had little more to offer. The inquisitors were anxious to conclude the case against Jorge de Almeida and to sentence him "in absentia".

The next several hours were spent in probing Luis' religious beliefs. His prodigious memory afforded him the opportunity to quote from the Thirteen Principles of Maimonides, the great Spanish Jewish philosopher of the 12th century. Luis also recited Psalms and the Ten Commandments, in Latin, as in Exodus and Deuteronomy, and even from the books of the Apocrypha.

Peralta, unyielding in his attitude toward Luis, was nevertheless impressed by the young man's intellectual prowess. The panel of priests, amazed at Luis' knowledgeability, understood how he could inspire others with his sincerity and strong passion. Deeply moved by his intelligence and strength of conviction, they were inclined to mercy rather than condemnation.

At the conclusion of the interrogation, Dr. Martos de Bohorques presented a lengthy indictment against Luis. In part, he stated, "Luis de Carvajal, *el Mozo*, is a 'relapso' who has abjured 'de vehementi' but has returned to the Old Religion like a dog that returns to its vomit." He continued with seething denunciations and accusations and then recommended that Luis be ordered relaxed to the authorities and the secular arm.

When asked if he had a final comment, Luis chose to retort to the term "dog" which he indicated "cannot be applied to someone who believes in the Law of God, which promises eternal life." He further stated, "I yearn to leave this prison and chains and go off to the heavens."

The panel of priests had hoped that Luis would break down and they could bring him back to Mother Church, not only for his ultimate salvation but also for the opportunity to plead for mercy on his behalf. They now expressed their hopes that this might still be accomplished.

"The business of the High Tribunal in this case is now concluded. The accused will appear for sentencing on a date determined by the Holy Office." Peralta made this statement with complete disregard for the priests' recommendations. He had accomplished what he had set out to do and now, at last, he would allow nothing to change that.

On the morning of October 2, 1596, Luis was summoned before the court. He was not aware that the sentences of his mother and sisters had already been reaffirmed. While his sentence was read, he stood like a statue, expressionless.

"Whereas we the Inquisitors against heretical wickedness and apostasy in this City of Mexico, in the States and Provinces of New Spain, and the district thereof, by apostolic and ordinary authority, having examined the record of the criminal proceedings instituted and prosecuted before us, between parties, on the one side Doctor Martos de Bohorques, the prosecuting attorney for this Holy Office, and on the other, Luis de Carvajal, *el Mozo*, charged with the crimes of heresy and apostasy because he had forsaken Our Holy Catholic Faith and relapsed into the observance of the dead Law of Moses, awaiting the coming of the Messiah promised by the said Law, and keeping and observing all the rites and ceremonies of the same...and whereas full and attentive consideration has been given by us to all the facts and merits of the case, and a consultation was held by us with persons of learning and righteous conscience, who might aid us with their prudent advice in reaching the proper decision:

"*Christo nomine invocato:*"

"We have, therefore, ordered, adjudged and decreed, and by these presents do order, adjudge and decree, that the case as presented and made by the prosecuting attorney for this Holy Office has been well made and substantiated and proved and we do hereby declare Luis de Carvajal, *el Mozo*, to be a heretic and a 'Judaizante', and an apostate against our Holy Catholic Faith, subject therefore to all the censures and penalties to which heretics and apostates are subject under the law...." The declaration continued at great length and finally ordered, "that he be surrendered to the secular authority for the punishment which may be provided by law and all his properties be confiscated."

The work of the Inquisition was now done in this case.

After the sentencing, Luis was returned to his cell, accompanied by Father Contreras who was assigned to stay at his side. It was hoped that Luis' conversion was still a possibility. The priest pleaded with him to re-embrace the Catholic faith but Luis answered, "I wish to die for the Almighty who handed down the Law to Moses. I have spent my short life defending that Law, even to the death — a small price to pay for precious salvation. My fervent wish is to be remembered by my people as a great teacher and restorer of the Law and that I defied the fires of the Inquisition for God, Adonai."

CHAPTER XXVI

PATH TO PARADISE

December eighth, 1596, the holy day called the Feast of the Immaculate Conception, was the day Peralta and Guerrero chose for the auto-da-fe in which Luis, his mother and three of his sisters, among others, were to be turned over to the secular authority. Peralta was determined that this day would be something special and impressive. Population control was an important issue for the Church; that is, control in the sense of promoting and maintaining Catholicism, not only as the primary religion but as the only religion.

On this day, there would be paraded before the populace, bigamists, Protestants, sorceresses, blasphemers and relapsers — and anybody else whose actions were deemed heretical. Peralta envisioned a magnificent spectacle displaying the power and influence of the Church. Elaborate preparations were made. For weeks, carpenters and tradesmen labored long hours to satisfy the instructions that their work must be "the finest ever."

Canopies were erected in the square so that the sun would not shine directly upon the proceedings, to keep the atmosphere somber. Steps leading up to a dais were built and carpeted. There the inquisitors and visiting dignitaries would be seated. Huge white crosses and silver candelabra adorned the tables and posts.

Around the perimeter of the square, as in an amphitheatre, were tiers of seats for the spectators. Off to the farthest corner, stood the "*quemadero*" — the burning place — where posts had been erected to which the condemned would be tied, each stake having its own pile of twigs, sticks or branches beneath it.

The event had been well publicized. People began arriving early in the morning to get the coveted seats, and those who were less fortunate stood along the outer boundaries. By midday, a mass of human beings crowded into the area, dressed in their colorful Sunday best, carrying bundles or boxes of food and containers of liquids, sustenance for the long day's proceedings. Those living in the immediate vicinity were hanging over railings of balconies, adding to the clatter, voices raised. Even though this was a holy day, a solemn one, the anticipation of the spectacle made it a day of celebration. All the while, a church choir stood nearby singing hymns.

The procession of attending dignitaries was impressive and awe-inspiring to the throngs who milled about. Cheers went up as the endless parade of monks and priests and the inquisitors passed by, dressed in their long, black robes with their high, black hats framing their solemn demeanors. Accompanying the representatives of the Church was the guest of honor, the Archbishop of the Philippines, the Franciscan friar Ignacio de Santibanez, together with Licentiate Vasco Lopez de Bibero, magistrate of Mexico City, many officials of the royal treasury, the military, and justices and officers of the "audiencia."

Father Contreras had gone to Luis' cell early that morning to tell him the news. The de Carvajals and other sentenced prisoners had been informed of the auto-da-fe the night before but Luis was the last to learn of it on that very day.

"Luis, the High Tribunal has ordered that you appear today for sentencing by the secular authorities."

Taken by surprise, Luis was speechless for several moments. In a resolute voice, he said, "Padre, I am ready. I have made my peace with God."

Father Conteras looked at the young man and pleaded, "Luis, I beg of you. Let us talk before you face your accusers. Let me show you the path to salvation," he persisted. But Luis remained obstinate. When it was time to leave the cell, Luis dropped to his knees and repeated the words he had written in his Will, a supplication to the Almighty: "My Lord, look upon me with grace, so that it may be known and seen in this kingdom and upon all the earth that Thou art our God and that Thine almighty and holy name, Adonai, is invoked with truth in Israel and among Israel's descendants. I commit this soul that Thou gavest me to Thy holy hands, promising with Thy help not to change my faith till death, nor after it."

The priest, deeply moved but not deterred, kept urging Luis as he led him from the jail to accept the Evangelical Law of Jesus Christ.

Sixty-seven prisoners were marched, barefoot, from their dungeons to the square in front of the Holy Office. Mobs of people followed behind and alongside, yelling obscenities and screaming for the condemned to convert. They threw vegetables and fruits at them and mocked their attire. Those at the end of the line, the "relapsos" and "dogmatizers", suffered the most abuse. All, except the blasphemers whose tongues were tied with rags, wore pointed hats painted with picture of flames, the flames of hell — the eternal torment — and "sanbenitos" embroidered with the cross of St. Andrew.

Ropes were tied around their necks and many were in chains. They carried crosses and the green candles that signified the hope for their salvation.

In a small wagon drawn by a donkey were Francisca, Catalina, Isabel, and Leonor. In another stood Manuel de Lucena and members of his family. In the back of the procession, barefoot, hatless, and in "sanbenito" — the only one not carrying a cross — was Luis, seated upon a donkey. Behind him were the effigies of those who could not be apprehended, either because they had died or had left the country. They would be tried "*en estatua*" (in effigy).

When Luis saw his loved ones, he could barely contain himself. Shouting over the clamor of the crowd, he offered spiritual strength. "My dear ones, have faith. The Lord will grant you great glory." He choked up and fell silent when Francisca, who recognized his voice above the din, let out a heart-rending scream as she turned to look into the face of her beloved son. His sisters, with tears overflowing, tried to manage brave expressions but quickly turned away from the pain so clearly etched upon their brother's face.

There is no degree of sadness comparable to the depths of despair that Luis felt as he watched his mother and sisters being jostled along in the crude, rough-hewn wooden wagon, jeered by the onlookers, insulted, and denigrated. *Poor Isabel*, he noticed, *so weak and debilitated, and brave Catalina and Leonor trying to comfort their sobbing mother.* He could hear her crying out to God, "*Senor, miserere mei y mi hijos!*" ("Have pity on me and my children!") The priest who accompanied them kept insisting, "Take the cross. Heaven will be your reward."

When all seventy-six reached the platform and were seated according to their "crimes", with Luis sitting on the top tier, a solemn oath was recited on behalf of the observers present. This was followed by a sermon preached by the Archbishop of Santibanez, reaffirming and defending the Holy Office in its pursuit of heretics.

The prisoners, one by one, were identified and their sentences read. With priests at their side, several of them who were arrested for the first time were given the opportunity to "return to Mother Church." Among them were Justa Mendez, her mother Clara, her brother Ricardo and Luis' brother-in-law Antonio de Caceres. They abjured "de vehementi" and were re-embraced by the Church. Luis gazed upon them with deep but controlled emotion. He took heart in knowing that they would keep the faith and continue to worship in secret. His teachings would live on, even though he would not.

Luis was the last to be sentenced. The Magistrate Licentiate de Bibero imposed the following: "Whereas the said Luis de Carvajal convicted by the Holy Office of the crimes imputed to him, and surrendered to me as the secular authority, for the proper action, was adjudged by the said Holy Office to be guilty as indicted...I do hereby condemn him to be burned at the stake, the penalty established by law in such cases, on this eighth day of December 1596, the Feast of the Immaculate Conception."

Father Contreras, standing next to Luis when the sentence was read, reflected, *Luis stands strong like a column of marble. His wan, handsome face betrays no emotion.* The priest marveled at his control.

Luis listened to the same sentencing for his beloved mother and siblings and some of his closest friends. He was resigned that their martyrdom was God's will.

The priest continued to plead and exhort but nothing could move Luis. In his final comments to Father Contreras, he said, "Father, I see many here today, even my own flesh and blood, yielding to the fear of violence, torture, and the bonfire. On this terrible day, in my last moments, the salvation of my soul is more important to me than the preservation of my life. Before I would betray God, I would give that life willingly. This is the only road to the glory of Paradise; there is none other."

Luis watched as his mother, Leonor, Catalina, and Isabel took the cross at the last minute so that they would be "mercifully" garroted before the fire was torched. In the midst of their peril, each called out to Luis, begging him to do the same. He closed his eyes and silently prayed for their souls.

"Luis, listen to your loved ones. Take the cross," the priest urged.

"No, I will not be garroted like a wretch on a gibbet. I shall go alive in live fire that I may have the greater reward."

The yelling of the crowd reached frenzied proportions. Their frustration that this prize might not be won was equal to that felt by the inquisitors and other dignitaries.

As Father Contreras walked with Luis to the *quemadero*, he continued to pursue theological arguments, trying to convince Luis to convert.

Luis remained unyielding. As they bound him to the stake, the last words upon his lips were "Sh'ma Yisra'el, Hear O Israel, the Lord is Our God, the Lord is one..."

* * *

AFTER THE FLAMES

One year later, in submitting his report on the auto-da-fe, Father Contreras wrote of Luis: "He was always such a good Jew and he reconciled his understanding, which was very profound and sensitive, with his highly inspired Divine determination to defend the Law of God — the Mosaic — and to fight for it. I have no doubt that if he had lived before the Incarnation of our Redeemer, he would have been a heroic Hebrew and his name would have been as famous in the Bible as are the names of those who died in defense of their law when it was necessary."